Charlotte Mary Yonge
**Aunt Charlotte's Greek History**

Yonge, Charlotte Mary

**Aunt Charlotte's Greek History**

ISBN/EAN: 978-3-86741-388-6
First published in 2010 by Europaeischer Hochschulverlag GmbH & Co KG, Bremen, Germany.

© Europaeischer Hochschulverlag GmbH & Co KG, Fahrenheitstr. 1, D-28359 Bremen (www.ehv-online.com). All rights reserved.

This book is a reproduction of an out of print title and has originally been published in 1876. Because no electronic master copies of this title could be obtained, the publisher had to reuse old copies of the text. We therefore apologize for any possible loss in quality.

Charlotte Mary Yonge

**Aunt Charlotte's Greek History**

## PREFACE.

In this little book the attempt has been to trace Greek History so as to be intelligible to young children. In fact, it will generally be found that classical history is remembered at an earlier age than modern history, probably because the events are simple, and there was something childlike in the nature of all the ancient Greeks. I would begin a child's reading with the History of England, as that which requires to be known best; but from this I should think it better to pass to the History of Greece, and that of Rome (which is in course of preparation), both because of their giving some idea of the course of time, and bringing Scripture history into connection with that of the world, and because little boys ought not to begin their classical studies without some idea of their bearing. I have begun with a few of the Greek myths, which are absolutely necessary to the understanding of both the history and of art. As to the names, the ordinary reading of them has been most frequently adopted, and the common Latin titles of the gods and goddesses have been used, because these, by long use, have really come to be their English names, and English literature at least will be better understood by calling the king of Olympus Jupiter, than by becoming familiar with him first as Zeus.

CHARLOTTE M. YONGE.

ORPHEUS

## CONTENTS.

| | |
|---|---:|
| CHAP. I. – OLYMPUS. | 1 |
| CHAP. II. – LIGHT AND DARK. | 6 |
| CHAP. III. – THE PEOPLING OF GREECE. | 13 |
| CHAP. IV. – THE HERO PERSEUS. | 19 |
| CHAP. V. – THE LABOURS OF HERCULES. | 24 |
| CHAP. VI. – THE ARGONAUTS. | 31 |
| CHAP. VII. – THE SUCCESS OF THE ARGONAUTS. | 37 |
| CHAP. VIII. – THE CHOICE OF PARIS. | 43 |
| CHAP. IX. – THE SIEGE OF TROY. | 49 |
| CHAP. X. – THE WANDERINGS OF ULYSSES. | 55 |
| CHAP. XI. – THE DOOM OF THE ATRIDES. | 61 |
| CHAP. XII. – AFTER THE HEROIC AGE. | 66 |
| CHAP. XIII. – LYCURGUS AND THE LAWS OF SPARTA. b.c. 884–668. | 72 |
| CHAP. XIV. – SOLON AND THE LAWS OF ATHENS. b.c. 594–546. | 77 |
| CHAP. XV. – PISISTRATUS AND HIS SONS. b.c. 558–499. | 83 |
| CHAP. XVI. – THE BATTLE OF MARATHON. b.c. 490. | 89 |
| CHAP. XVII. – THE EXPEDITION OF XERXES. b.c. 480. | 94 |
| CHAP. XVIII. – THE BATTLE OF PLATÆA. b.c. 479–460. | 100 |
| CHAP. XIX. – THE AGE OF PERICLES. b.c. 464–429. | 106 |
| CHAP. XX. – THE EXPEDITION TO SICILY. b.c. 415–413. | 112 |
| CHAP. XXI. – THE SHORE OF THE GOAT'S RIVER. b.c. 406–402. | 117 |
| CHAP. XXII. – THE RETREAT OF THE TEN THOUSAND. b.c. 402–399. | 122 |
| CHAP. XXIII. – THE DEATH OF SOCRATES. b.c. 399. | 127 |

| | |
|---|---|
| CHAP. XXIV. – THE SUPREMACY OF SPARTA. b.c. 396. | 133 |
| CHAP. XXV. – THE TWO THEBAN FRIENDS. b.c. 387-362. | 138 |
| CHAP. XXVI. – PHILIP OF MACEDON. b.c. 364. | 143 |
| CHAP. XXVII. – THE YOUTH OF ALEXANDER. b.c. 356-334. | 148 |
| CHAP. XXVIII. – THE EXPEDITION TO PERSIA. b.c. 334. | 154 |
| CHAP. XXIX. ALEXANDER'S EASTERN CONQUESTS. b.c. 331-328. | 159 |
| CHAP. XXX. – THE END OF ALEXANDER. b.c. 328. | 164 |
| CHAP. XXXI. THE LAST STRUGGLES OF ATHENS. b.c. 334-311. | 169 |
| CHAP. XXXII. – THE FOUR NEW KINGDOMS. b.c. 311-287. | 174 |
| CHAP. XXXIII – PYRRHUS, KING OF EPIRUS. b.c. 287. | 179 |
| CHAP. XXXIV. ARATUS AND THE ACHAIAN LEAGUE. b.c. 267. | 184 |
| CHAP. XXXV. AGIS AND THE REVIVAL OF SPARTA. b.c. 244-236. | 189 |
| CHAP. XXXVI. CLEOMENES AND THE FALL OF SPARTA. b.c.236-222. | 194 |
| CHAP. XXXVII. PHILOPŒMEN, THE LAST OF THE GREEKS. b.c. 236-184. | 199 |
| CHAP. XXXVIII. – THE FALL OF GREECE. b.c. 189-146. | 204 |
| CHAP. XXXIX. – THE GOSPEL IN GREECE. b.c. 146-a.d. 60. | 209 |
| CHAP. XL. – UNDER THE ROMAN EMPIRE. | 215 |
| CHAP. XLI. – THE FRANK CONQUEST. 1201-1446. | 220 |
| CHAP. XLII. – THE TURKISH CONQUEST. 1453-1670. | 225 |
| CHAP. XLIII. THE VENETIAN CONQUEST AND LOSS. 1684-1796. | 229 |
| CHAP. XLIV. – THE WAR OF INDEPENDENCE. 1815. | 234 |
| CHAP. XLV. – THE KINGDOM OF GREECE. 1822-1875. | 239 |

MOUNT OLYMPUS.

## CHAP. I. — OLYMPUS.

I am going to tell you the history of the most wonderful people who ever lived. But I have to begin with a good deal that is not true; for the people who descended from Japhet's son Javan, and lived in the beautiful islands and peninsulas called Greece, were not trained in the knowledge of God like the Israelites, but had to guess for themselves. They made strange stories, partly from the old beliefs they brought from the east, partly from their ways of speaking of the powers of nature — sky, sun, moon, stars, and clouds — as if they were real beings, and so again of good or bad qualities as beings also, and partly from old stories about their forefathers. These stories got mixed up with their belief, and came to be part of their religion and history; and they wrote beautiful poems about them, and made such lovely statues in their honour, that nobody can understand anything about art or learning who has not learnt these stories. I must begin with trying to tell you a few of them.

HEAD OF JUPITER.

In the first place, the Greeks thought there were twelve greater gods and goddesses who lived in Olympus. There is really a mountain called Olympus, and those who lived far from it thought it went up into the sky, and that the gods really dwelt on the top of it. Those who lived near, and knew they did not, thought they lived in the sky. But the chief of all, the father of gods and men, was the sky-god — Zeus, as the Greeks called him, or Jupiter, as he was called in Latin. However, as all things are born of Time, so the sky or Jupiter was said to have a father, Time, whose Greek name was Kronos. His other name was Saturn; and as Time devours his offspring, so Saturn was said to have had the bad habit of eating up his children as fast as they were born, till at last his wife Rhea contrived to give him a stone in swaddling clothes, and while he was biting this hard morsel, Jupiter was saved from him, and afterwards two other sons, Neptune (Poseidon) and Pluto (Hades), who became lords of the ocean and of the world of the spirits of the dead; for on the sea and on death Time's tooth has no power. However, Saturn's reign was thought to have been a very peaceful and happy one. For as people always think of the days of Paradise, and believe that the days of old were better than their own times, so the Greeks thought there had been four ages — the

Golden age, the Silver age, the Brazen age, and the Iron age — and that people had been getting worse in each of them. Poor old Saturn, after the Silver age, had had to go into retirement, with only his own star, the planet Saturn, left to him; and Jupiter was reigning now, on his throne on Olympus, at the head of the twelve greater gods and goddesses, and it was the Iron age down below. His star, the planet we still call by his name, was much larger and brighter than Saturn. Jupiter was always thought of by the Greeks as a majestic-looking man in his full strength, with thick hair and beard, and with lightnings in his hand and an eagle by his side. These lightnings or thunderbolts were forged by his crooked son Vulcan (Hephæstion), the god of fire, the smith and armourer of Olympus, whose smithies were in the volcanoes (so called from his name), and whose workmen were the Cyclops or Round Eyes — giants, each with one eye in the middle of his forehead. Once, indeed, Jupiter had needed his bolts, for the Titans, a horrible race of monstrous giants, of whom the worst was Briareus, who had a hundred hands, had tried, by piling up mountains one upon the other, to scale heaven and throw him down; but when Jupiter was hardest pressed, a dreadful pain in his head caused him to bid Vulcan to strike it with his hammer. Then out darted Heavenly Wisdom, his beautiful daughter Pallas Athene or Minerva, fully armed, with piercing, shining eyes, and by her counsels he cast down the Titans, and heaped their own mountains, Etna and Ossa and Pelion, on them to keep them down; and whenever there was an earthquake, it was thought to be caused by one of these giants struggling to get free, though perhaps there was some remembrance of the tower of Babel in the story. Pallas, this glorious daughter of Jupiter, was wise, brave, and strong, and she was also the goddess of women's works — of all spinning, weaving, and sewing.

Jupiter's wife, the queen of heaven or the air, was Juno — in Greek, Hera — the white-armed, ox-eyed, stately lady, whose bird was the peacock. Do you know how the peacock got the eyes in his tail? They once belonged to Argus, a shepherd with a hundred eyes, whom Juno had set to watch a cow named Io, who was really a lady, much hated by her. Argus watched till Mercury (Hermes) came and lulled him to sleep with soft music, and then drove Io away. Juno was so angry, that she caused all the eyes to be taken from Argus and put into her peacock's tail.

Mercury has a planet called after him too, a very small one, so close to the sun that we only see it just after sunset or before sunrise. I believe Mercury or Hermes really meant the morning breeze. The story went that he was born early in the morning in a cave, and after he had slept a little while in his cradle, he came forth, and, finding the shell of a tortoise with some strings of the inwards stretched across it, he at once began to play on it, and thus formed the first lyre. He was so swift that he was the messenger of Jupiter, and he is always represented with wings on his cap and sandals; but as the wind not only makes music, but blows things away unawares, so Mercury came to be viewed not only as the god of fair speech, but as a terrible thief, and the god of thieves. You see, as long as these Greek stories are parables, they are grand and beautiful; but when the beings are looked on as like men, they are absurd and often horrid. The gods had another messenger, Iris, the rainbow, who always carried messages of mercy, a recollection of the bow in the clouds; but she chiefly belonged to Juno.

All the twelve greater gods had palaces on Olympus, and met every day in Jupiter's hall to feast on ambrosia, a sort of food of life which made them immortal. Their drink was nectar, which was poured into their golden cups at first by Vulcan, but he stumbled and hobbled so with his lame leg that they chose instead the fresh and graceful Hebe, the goddess of youth, till she was careless, and one day fell down, cup and nectar and all. The gods thought they must find another cupbearer, and, looking down, they saw a beautiful youth named Ganymede watching his flocks upon Mount Ida. So they sent Jupiter's eagle down to fly away with him and bring him up to Olympus. They gave him some ambrosia to make him immortal, and established him as their cupbearer. Besides this, the gods were thought to feed on the smoke and smell of the sacrifices people offered up to them on earth, and always to help those who offered them most sacrifices of animals and incense.

The usual names of these twelve were — Jupiter, Neptune, Juno, Latona, Apollo, Diana, Pallas, Venus, Vulcan, Mercury, Vesta, and Ceres; but there were multitudes besides — "gods many and lords many" of all sorts of different dignities. Every river had its god, every mountain and wood was full of nymphs, and there was a great god of all nature called Pan, which in Greek means All. Neptune was only a visitor in Olympus, though he had a right there. His kingdom was the sea, which he ruled with his trident, and where he had a whole world of lesser gods and nymphs, tritons and sea horses, to attend upon his chariot.

And the quietest and best of all the goddesses was Vesta, the goddess of the household hearth — of home, that is to say. There are no stories to be told about her, but a fire was always kept burning in her honour in each city, and no one might tend it who was not good and pure.

## CHAP. II. — LIGHT AND DARK.

The god and goddess of light were the glorious twin brother and sister, Phœbus Apollo and Diana or Artemis. They were born in the isle of Delos, which was caused to rise out of the sea to save their mother, Latona, from the horrid serpent, Python, who wanted to devour her. Gods were born strong and mighty; and the first thing Apollo did was to slay the serpent at Delphi with his arrows. Here was a dim remembrance of the promise that the Seed of the woman should bruise the serpent's head, and also a thought of the way Light slays the dragon of darkness with his beams. Apollo was lord of the day, and Diana queen of the night. They were as bright and pure as the thought of man could make them, and always young. The beams or rays were their arrows, and so Diana was a huntress, always in the woods with her nymphs; and she was so modest, that once, when an unfortunate wanderer, named Actæon, came on her with her nymphs by chance when they were bathing in a stream, she splashed some water in his face and turned him into a stag, so that his own dogs gave chase to him and killed him. I am afraid Apollo and Diana were rather cruel; but the darting rays of the sun and moon kill sometimes as well as bless; and so they were the senders of all sharp, sudden strokes. There was a queen called Niobe, who had six sons and daughters so bright and fair that she boasted that they were equal to Apollo and Diana, which made Latona so angry, that she sent her son and daughter to slay them all with their darts. The unhappy Niobe, thus punished for her impiety, wept a river of tears till she was turned into stone.

SUPPOSED TEMPLE OF JUPITER PANHELLENIUS IN AEGINA.

The moon belonged to Diana, and was her car; the sun, in like manner, to Apollo, though he did not drive the car himself, but Helios, the sun-god, did. The world was thought to be a flat plate, with Delphi in the middle, and the ocean all round. In the far east the lady dawn, Aurora, or Eôs, opened the gates with her rosy fingers, and out came the golden car of the sun, with glorious white horses driven by Helios, attended by the Hours strewing dew and flowers. It passed over the arch of the heavens to the ocean again on the west, and there Aurora met it again in fair colours, took out the horses, and let them feed. Aurora had married a man named Tithonus. She gave him ambrosia, which made him immortal, but she could not keep him from growing old, so he became smaller and smaller, till he dwindled into a grasshopper, and at last only his voice was to be heard chirping at sunrise and sunset.

Helios had an earthly wife too, and a son named Phaëton, who once begged to be allowed to drive the chariot of the sun for just one day. Helios yielded; but poor Phaëton had no strength nor skill to guide the horses in the right curve. At one moment they rushed to the earth and scorched the trees, at another they flew up to heaven and would have burnt Olympus, if Jupiter had not cast his thunderbolts at the rash driver and hurled him down into a river, where he was drowned. His sisters wept till they were changed into poplar trees, and their tears hardened into amber drops.

Mercury gave his lyre to Apollo, who was the true god of music and poetry, and under him were nine nymphs — the Muses, daughters of memory — who dwelt on Mount Parnassus, and were thought to inspire all noble and heroic song, all poems in praise to or of the gods or of brave men, and the graceful music and dancing at their feasts, also the knowledge of the stars of earth and heaven.

HEAD OF PALLAS.

These three — Apollo, Diana, and Pallas — were the gods of all that was nobly, purely, and wisely lovely; but the Greeks also believed in powers of ill, and there was a goddess of beauty, called Venus (Aphrodite). Such beauty was hers as is the mere prettiness and charm of pleasure — nothing high or fine. She was said to have risen out of the sea, as the sunshine touched the waves, with her golden hair dripping with the spray; and her favourite home was in myrtle groves, where she drove her car, drawn by doves, attended by the three Graces, and by multitudes of little winged children, called Loves; but there was generally said to be one special son of hers, called Love — Cupid in Latin, Eros in Greek — whose arrows, when tipped with gold, made people fall in love, and when tipped with lead, made them hate one another. Her husband was the ugly, crooked smith, Vulcan — perhaps because pretty ornaments come of the hard work of the smith; but she never behaved well to him, and only coaxed him when she wanted something that his clever hands could make.

She was much more fond of amusing herself with Mars (Ares), the god of war, another of the evil gods, for he was fierce, cruel, and violent, and where he went slaughter and blood were sure to follow him and his horrid daughter Bellona. His star was "the red planet Mars;" but Venus had the beautiful clear one, which, according as it is seen either at sunrise or sunset, is called the morning or evening star. Venus also loved a beautiful young earthly youth, called Adonis, who died of a thrust from a wild boar's tusk, while his blood stained crimson the pretty flower, pheasant's eye, which is still called Adonis. Venus was so wretched that she persuaded Jupiter to decree that Adonis should come back and live for one-half of the year, but he was to go down to Pluto's underground kingdom the other half. This is because plants and flowers are beautiful for one year, die down, and rise again.

TRIPTOLEMUS.

But there is a much prettier story, with something of the same meaning, about Ceres (Demeter), the grave, motherly goddess of corn and all the fruits of the earth. She had one fair daughter, named Proserpine (Persephone), who was playing with her companions near Mount Etna, gathering flowers in the meadows, when grim old Pluto pounced upon her and carried her off into his underground world to be his bride. Poor Ceres did not know what had become of her darling, and wandered up and down the world seeking for her, tasting no food or drink, till at last, quite spent, she was taken in as a poor woman by Celeus, king of Eleusis, and became nurse to his infant child Triptolemus. All Eleusis was made rich with corn, while no rain fell and no crops grew on the rest of the earth; and though first Iris and then all the gods came to beg Ceres to relent, she would grant nothing unless she had her daughter back. So Jupiter sent Mercury to bring Proserpine home; but she was only to be allowed to stay on earth on condition that she had eaten nothing while in the under world. Pluto, knowing this, had made her eat half a pomegranate, and so she could not stay with her mother; but Ceres's tears prevailed so far that she was to spend the summer above ground and the winter below. For she really was the flowers and fruit. Ceres had grown so

10

fond of little Triptolemus that she wanted to make him immortal; but, as she had no ambrosia, this could only be done by putting him on the fire night after night to burn away his mortal part. His mother looked in one night during the operation, and shrieked so that she prevented it; so all Ceres could do for him was to give him grains of wheat and a dragon car, with which he travelled all about the world, teaching men to sow corn and reap harvests.

Proserpine seems to have been contented in her underground kingdom, where she ruled with Pluto. It was supposed to be below the volcanic grounds in southern Italy, near Lake Avernus. The entrance to it was guarded by a three-headed dog, named Cerberus, and the way to it was barred by the River Styx. Every evening Mercury brought all the spirits of the people who had died during the day to the shore of the Styx, and if their funeral rites had been properly performed, and they had a little coin on the tongue to pay the fare, Charon, the ferryman, took them across; but if their corpses were in the sea, or on battle-fields, unburied, the poor shades had to flit about vainly begging to be ferried over. After they had crossed, they were judged by three judges, and if they had been wicked, were sent over the river of fire to be tormented by the three Furies, Alecto, Megara, and Tisiphone, who had snakes as scourges and in their hair. If they had been brave and virtuous, they were allowed to live among beautiful trees and flowers in the Elysian fields, where Pluto reigned; but they seem always to have longed after the life they had lost; and these Greek notions of bliss seem sad besides what we know to be the truth. Here, too, lived the three Fates, always spinning the threads of men's lives; Clotho held the distaff, Lachesis drew out the thread, and Atropos with her shears cut it off when the man was to die. And, though Jupiter was mighty, nothing could happen but by Fate, which was stronger than he.

MARS AND VICTORY.

## CHAP. III. — THE PEOPLING OF GREECE.

You remember the Titans who rebelled against Jupiter. There was one who was noble, and wise, and kind, who did not rebel, and kept his brother from doing so. His name was Prometheus, which means Forethought; his brother's was Epimetheus, or Afterthought; their father was Iapetus. When all the other Titans had been buried under the rocks, Jupiter bade Prometheus mould men out of the mud, and call on the winds of heaven to breathe life into them. Then Prometheus loved the beings he had made, and taught them to build houses, and tame the animals, and row and sail on the sea, and study the stars. But Zeus was afraid they would be too mighty, and would not give them fire. Then Prometheus climbed the skies, and brought fire down for them in a hollow reed.

The gods were jealous, and thought it time to stop this. So Jupiter bade Vulcan mould a woman out of clay, and Pallas to adorn her with all charms and gifts, so that she was called Pandora, or All Gifts; and they gave her a casket, into which they had put all pains, and griefs, and woes, and ills, and nothing good in it but hope; and they sent her down to visit the two Titan brothers. Prometheus knew that Jupiter hated them, and he had warned Epimetheus not to take any gift that came from Olympus; but he was gone from home when Pandora came; and when Epimetheus saw how lovely she was, and heard her sweet voice, he was won over to trust her, and to open the box. Then out flew all the evils and miseries that were stored in it, and began to torment poor mankind with war, and sickness, and thirst, and hunger, and nothing good was left but hope at the bottom of the box. And by-and-by there came spirits, called Prayers, but they were lame, coming after evil, because people are so apt not to begin to pray till harm has befallen them.

MOUNT PARNASSUS.

The gods undertook also to accept sacrifices, claiming a share in whatever animal man slew. Prometheus guarded his people here by putting the flesh of a bullock on one side, and the bones and inward parts covered with the fat on the other, and bidding Jupiter choose which should be his. The fat looked as if the heap it covered were the best, and Jupiter chose that, and was forced to abide by his choice; so that, whenever a beast was killed for food, the bones and fat were burnt on the altar, and man had the flesh. All this made Jupiter so angry, that, as Prometheus was immortal and could not be killed, he chained the great, good Titan to a rock on Mount Caucasus, and sent an eagle continually to rend his side and tear out his liver as fast as it grew again; but Prometheus, in all his agony, kept hope, for he knew that deliverance would come to him; and, in the meantime, he was still the comforter and counsellor of all who found their way to him.

Men grew very wicked, owing to the evils in Pandora's box, and Jupiter resolved to drown them all with a flood; but Prometheus, knowing it beforehand, told his mortal son Deucalion to build a ship and store it with all sorts of food. In it Deucalion and his wife Pyrrha floated about for nine days till all men had been drowned, and as the waters went down the ship rested on Mount Parnassus, and Deucalion and Pyrrha came out and offered sacrifices to Jupiter. He was appeased, and sent Mercury down to ask what he should grant them. Their prayer was that the earth might be filled again with people, upon which the god bade them walk up the hill and throw behind them the bones of their grandmother. Now Earth was said to be the mother of the Titans, so the bones of their grandmother were the rocks, so as they went they picked up stones and threw them over their shoulders. All those that Deucalion threw rose up as men, and all those that Pyrrha threw became women, and thus the earth was alive again with human beings. No one can fail to see what far older histories must have been brought in the minds of the Greeks, and have been altered into these tales, which have much beauty in themselves. The story of the flood seems to have been mixed up with some small later inundation which only affected Greece.

The proper old name of Greece was Hellas, and the people whom we call Greeks called themselves Hellênes. [1] Learned men know that they, like all the people of Europe, and also the Persians and Hindoos, sprang from one great family of the sons of Japhet, called Arians. A tribe called Pelasgi came first, and lived in Asia Minor, Greece, and Italy; and after them came the Hellênes, who were much quicker and cleverer than the Pelasgi, and became their masters in most of Greece. So that the people we call Greeks were a mixture of the two, and they were divided into three lesser tribes — the Æolians, Dorians, and Ionians.

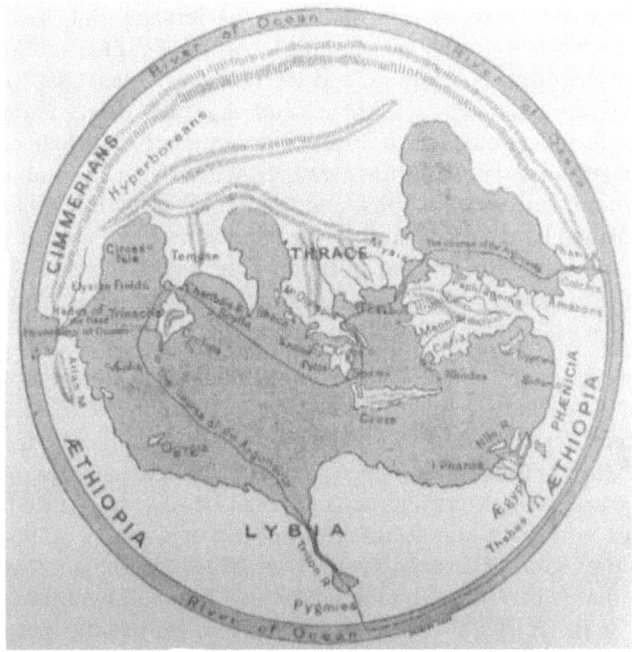

Now, having told you that bit of truth, I will go back to what the Greeks thought. They said that Deucalion had a son whose name was Hellên, and that he again had three sons, called Æolus, Dorus, and Xuthus. Æolus was the father of the Æolian Greeks, and some in after times thought that he was the same with the god called Æolus, who was thought to live in the Lipari Islands; and these keep guard over the spirits of the winds — Boreas, the rough, lively north wind; Auster, the rainy south wind; Eurus, the bitter east; and Zephyr, the gentle west. He kept them in a cave, and let one out according to the way the wind was wanted to blow, or if there was to be a storm he sent out two at once to struggle, and fight, and roar together, and lash up Neptune's world, the sea. The Æolians did chiefly live in the islands and at Corinth. One of the sons of Æolus turned out very badly, and cheated Jupiter. His name was Sisyphus, and he was punished in Tartarus — Pluto's world below — by having always to roll a stone up a mountain so steep that it was sure to come down upon him again.

Dorus was, of course, the father of the Dorians; and Xuthus had a son, called Iôn, who was the father of the Ionians. But, besides all these, there was a story of two brothers, named Ægyptus and Danaus, one of whom settled in Egypt, and the other in Argos. One had fifty sons and the other fifty daughters, and Ægyptus decreed that they should all marry; but Danaus and his daughters hated their cousins, and the father gave each bride a dagger, with which she stabbed her bridegroom. Only one had pity, and though the other forty-nine were not punished here, yet, when they died and went to Tartarus, they did not escape, but were obliged to be for ever trying to carry water in bottomless vessels. The people of Argos called themselves Danai, and no doubt some of them came from Egypt.

One more story, and a very strange one, tells of the peopling of Greece. A fair lady, named Europa, was playing in the meadows on the Phœnician coast, when a great white bull came to her, let his horns be wreathed with flowers, lay down, and invited her to mount his back; but no sooner had she done so, than he rose and trotted down with her to the sea, and swam with her out of sight. He took her, in fact, to the island of Crete, where her son Minos was so good and just a king, that, when he died, Pluto appointed him and two others to be judges of the spirits of the dead. Europe was called after Europa, as the loss of her led settlers there from Asia. Europa's family grieved for her, and her father, mother, and brother went everywhere in search of her. Cadmus was the name of her brother, and he and his mother went far and wide, till the mother died, and Cadmus went to Delphi — the place thought to be the centre of the earth — where Apollo had slain the serpent Python, and where he had a temple and cavern in which every question could be answered. Such places of divination were called oracles, and Cadmus was here told to cease from seeking his sister, and to follow a cow till she fell down with fatigue, and to build a city on that spot. The poor cow went till she came into Bœotia, and there fell. Cadmus meant to offer her up, and went to fetch water from a fountain near, but as he stooped a fierce dragon rushed on him. He had a hard fight to kill it, but Pallas shone out in her beauty on him, and bade him sow its teeth in the ground. He did so, and they sprung up as warriors, who at once began to fight, and killed one another, all but five, who made friends, and helped Cadmus to build the famous city called Thebes. It is strange, after so wild a story as this, to be told that Cadmus first taught writing in Greece, and brought the alphabet of sixteen letters. The Greek alphabet was really learnt from the Phœnicians, and most likely the whole is a curious story of some settlement of that eastern people in Greece. Most likely they brought in the worship of the wine-god, Bacchus (Dionysos), for he was called Cadmus's grandson. An orphan at first, he was brought up by the nymphs and Mercury, and then became a great conqueror, going to India, and Egypt, and everywhere, carrying the vine and teaching the use of wine. He was attended by an old fat man, named Silenus, and by creatures, called Fauns and Satyrs, like men with goats' ears and legs; his crown was of ivy, and his chariot was drawn by leopards, and he was at last raised to Olympus. His feasts were called orgies; he-goats were sacrificed at them, and songs were sung, after which there was much drinking, and people danced holding sticks wreathed with vine and ivy leaves. The women who danced were called Bacchanals. The better sort of Greeks at first would not adopt these shameful rites. There were horrid stories of women who refused them going mad and leaping into the sea, and the Bacchanals used to fall upon and destroy all who resisted them.

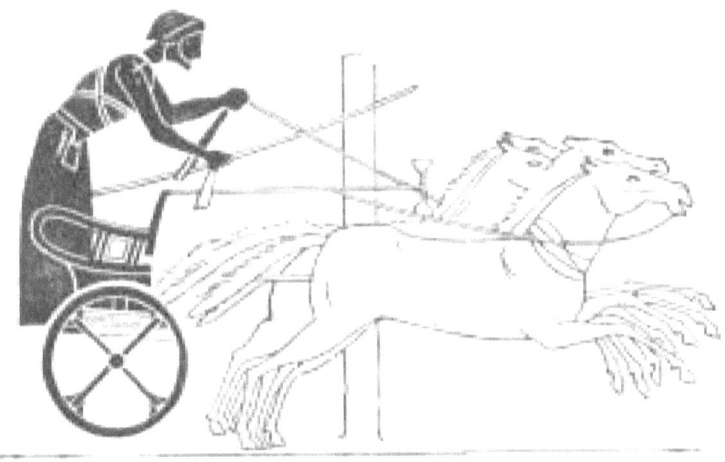

## CHAP. IV. — THE HERO PERSEUS.

A hero means a great and glorious man, and the Greeks thought they had many such among their forefathers — nay, that they were sons of gods, and themselves, after many trials and troubles, became gods, since these Greeks of old felt that "we are also His offspring."

Here is a story of one of these heroes. His mother was the daughter of an Argive king, and was named Danaë. He was named Perseus, and had bright eyes and golden hair like the morning. When he was a little babe, he and his mother were out at sea, and were cast on the isle of Seriphos, where a fisherman named Dictys took care of them. A cruel tyrant named Polydectes wanted Danaë to be his wife, and, as she would not consent, he shut her up in prison, saying that she should never come out till her son Perseus had brought him the head of the Gorgon Medusa, thinking he must be lost by the way. For the Gorgons were three terrible sisters, who lived in the far west beyond the setting sun. Two of them were immortal, and had dragon's wings and brazen claws and serpent hair, but their sister Medusa was mortal, and so beautiful in the face that she had boasted of being fairer than Pallas. To punish her presumption, her hair was turned to serpents, and whosoever looked on her face, sad and lovely as it was, would instantly be turned into stone.

But, for his mother's sake, young Perseus was resolved to dare this terrible adventure, and his bravery brought help from the gods. The last night before he was to set out Pallas came and showed him the images of the three Gorgons, and bade him not concern himself about the two he could not kill; but she gave him a mirror of polished brass, and told him only to look at Medusa's reflection on it, for he would become a stone if he beheld her real self. Then Mercury came and gave Perseus a sword of light that would cleave all on whom it might fall, lent him his own winged sandals, and told him to go first to the nymphs of the Graiæ, the Gorgons' sisters, and make them tell him the way.

So the young hero went by land and sea, still westwards, to the very borders of the world, where stands the giant of the west, Atlas, holding up the great vault of the skies on his broad shoulders. Beyond lay the dreary land of twilight, on the shores of the great ocean that goes round the world, and on the rocks on the shores sat the three old, old nymphs, the Graiæ, who had been born with grey hair, and had but one eye and one tooth among them, which they passed to one another in turn. When the first had seen the noble-looking youth speeding to them, she handed her eye on, that the next sister might look at him; but Perseus was too quick — he caught the one eye out of her hand, and then told the three poor old nymphs that he did not want to hurt them, but that he must keep their eye till they had told him the way to Medusa the Gorgon.

They told him the way, and, moreover, they gave him a mist-cap helmet from Tartarus, which would make him invisible whenever he put it on, and also a bag, which he slung on his back; and, thus armed, he went further to the very bounds of the world, and he took his mirror in his hand, and looked into it. There he saw the three Gorgon sisters, their necks covered with scales like those of snakes (at least those of two), their teeth like boar's tusks, their hands like brass, and their wings of gold; but they were all fast asleep, and Perseus, still looking into his mirror, cleft Medusa's neck with his all-cutting sword, and put her head into the bag on his back without ever seeing her face. Her sisters awoke and darted after him; but he put on his helmet of mist, and they lost him, while he fled away on Mercury's swift-winged sandals. As he sped eastward, he heard a voice asking whether he had really killed the Gorgon. It was Atlas, the old heaven-supporting giant; and when Perseus answered that he had, Atlas declared that he must see the head to convince him. So Perseus put a hand over his shoulder, and drew it up by its snaky hair; but no sooner had Atlas cast his eyes on it than he turned into a mountain, his white beard and hair becoming the snowy peak, and his garments the woods and forests. And there he still stands on the west coast of Africa, and all our modern map-books are named after him.

PERSEUS AND ANDROMEDA.

But Perseus' adventures were not over. As he flew on by the Lybian coast he heard a sound of wailing, and beheld a beautiful maiden chained by her hands and feet to a rock. He asked what had led her to this sad plight, and she answered that she was Andromeda, the daughter of Cepheus and Cassiopeia, king and queen of Ethiopia, and that her mother had foolishly boasted that she was fairer than the Nereids, the fifty nymphs who are the spirits of the waves. Neptune was so much displeased that he sent a flood to overflow the land, and a sea-monster to devour the people and cattle. In an oasis or isle of fertility in the middle of the Lybian desert was a temple of Jupiter, there called Ammon, and the Ethiopians had sent there to ask what to do. The oracle replied that the evil should cease if Andromeda were given up to the monster. Cepheus had been obliged to yield her up because of the outcries of the people, and here she was waiting to be devoured. Perseus, of course, was ready. He heard the monster coming, bade Andromeda close her eyes, and then held up the Gorgon's head. In an instant her foe had become a rock, and he cleft the maiden's chains, brought her back to her father and mother, who gave her to him in marriage, and made a great feast; but here a former lover of hers insulted them both so much, that Perseus was forced to show him the Gorgon's face, and turn him into stone.

Then Perseus, with Andromeda, took his way to Seriphos. Indeed it was high time that he should come back, for Polydectes, thinking that he must long ago have been turned into a rock at the sight of Medusa, had tried to take Danaë by force to be his wife, and she had fled into a temple, where no one dared to touch her, since it was always believed that the gods punished such as dragged suppliants away from their temples. So Perseus went to Polydectes, who was in the midst of a feast, and, telling him that his bidding was done, held up the head of Medusa, and of course the king and his whole court turned at once into stone. Now that the work of the Gorgon's head was done, Perseus offered it to Pallas, who placed it upon her shield, or, as it is always called, her ægis; and he gave back the sword of light, cap of mist, and winged sandals to Mercury.

After this he returned to Argos, and there, at a game of quoits, he had the misfortune to throw the quoit the wrong way, and hit his grandfather, the king, so as to kill him. Perseus reigned afterwards, and, like all the nobler Greek heroes, kept out the worship of Bacchus and its foul orgies from his dominions; but he afterwards exchanged kingdoms with another king, and built the city of Tiryas. He lived happily with Andromeda, and had a great many children, whose descendants viewed him as a demi-god, and had shrines to him, where they offered incense and sacrifice; for they thought that he and all the family were commemorated in the stars, and named the groups after them. You may find them all in the North. Andromeda is a great square, as if large stars marked the rivets of her chains on the rock; Perseus, a long curved cluster of bright stars, as if climbing up to deliver her; her mother Cassiopeia like a bright W, in which the Greeks traced a chair, where she sat with her back to the rest to punish her for her boast. Cepheus is there too, but he is smaller, and less easy to find. They are all in the North, round the Great Bear, who was said by the Greeks to be a poor lady whom Juno had turned into a bear, and who was almost killed unknowingly by her own son when out hunting. He is the Little Bear, with the pole star in his tail, and she is the Great Bear, always circling round him, and, as the Greeks used to say, never dipping her muzzle into the ocean, because she is so far north that she never sets.

This story of Perseus is a very old one, which all nations have loved to tell, though with different names. You will be amused to think that the old Cornish way of telling it is found in "Jack the Giant-Killer," who had seven-leagued boots and a cap of mist, and delivered fair ladies from their cruel foes.

CYCLOPEAN WALL.

## CHAP. V. — THE LABOURS OF HERCULES.

One morning Jupiter boasted among the gods in Olympus that a son would that day be born in the line of Perseus, who would rule over all the Argives. Juno was angry and jealous at this, and, as she was the goddess who presided over the births of children, she contrived to hinder the birth of the child he intended till that day was over, and to hasten that of another grandson of the great Perseus. This child was named Eurystheus, and, as he had been born on the right day, Jupiter was forced to let him be king of Argos, Sparta, and Mycenæ, and all the Dorian race; while the boy whom he had meant to be the chief was kept in subjection, in spite of having wonderful gifts of courage and strength, and a kind, generous nature, that always was ready to help the weak and sorrowful.

His name was Alcides, or Hercules, and he was so strong at ten months old, that, with his own hands, he strangled two serpents whom Juno sent to devour him in his cradle. He was bred up by Chiron, the chief of the Centaurs, a wondrous race of beings, who had horses' bodies as far as the forelegs, but where the neck of the horse would begin had human breasts and shoulders, with arms and heads. Most of them were fierce and savage; but Chiron was very wise and good, and, as Jupiter made him immortal, he was the teacher of many of the great Greek heroes. When Hercules was about eighteen, two maidens appeared to him — one in a simple white dress, grave, modest and seemly; the other scarcely clothed, but tricked out in ornaments, with a flushed face, and bold, roving eyes. The first told him that she was Virtue, and that, if he would follow her, she would lead him through many hard trials, but that he would be glorious at last, and be blest among the gods. The other was Vice, and she tried to wile him by a smooth life among wine-cups and dances and flowers and sports, all to be enjoyed at once. But the choice of Hercules was Virtue, and it was well for him, for Jupiter, to make up for Juno's cheat, had sworn that, if he fulfilled twelve tasks which Eurystheus should put upon him, he should be declared worthy of being raised to the gods at his death.

SCENE IN THE ARACHNAEAN MOUNTAINS NEAR ARGOS.

Eurystheus did not know that in giving these tasks he was making his cousin fulfil his course; but he was afraid of such a mighty man, and hoped that one of these would be the means of getting rid of him. So when he saw Hercules at Argos, with a club made of a forest tree in his hand, and clad in the skin of a lion which he had slain, Eurystheus bade him go and kill a far more terrible lion, of giant brood, and with a skin that could not be pierced, which dwelt in the valley of Nemea. The fight was a terrible one; the lion could not be wounded, and Hercules was forced to grapple with it, and strangle it in his arms. He lost a finger in the struggle, but at last the beast died in his grasp, and he carried it on his back to Argos, where Eurystheus was so much frightened at the grim sight that he fled away to hide himself, and commanded Hercules not to bring his monsters within the gates of the city.

There was a second labour ready for Hercules — namely, the destroying a serpent with nine heads, called Hydra, whose lair was the marsh of Lerna. Hercules went to the battle, and managed to crush one head with his club, but that moment two sprang up in its place; moreover, a huge crab came out of the swamp, and began to pinch his heels. Still he did not lose heart, but, calling his friend Iolaus, he bade him take a fire-brand and burn the necks as fast as he cut off the heads; and thus at last they killed the creature, and Hercules dipped his arrows in its poisonous blood, so that their least wound became fatal. Eurystheus said that it had not been a fair victory, since Hercules had been helped, and Juno put the crab into the skies as the constellation Cancer; while a labour to patience was next devised for Hercules — namely, the chasing of the Arcadian stag, which was sacred to Diana, and had golden horns and brazen hoofs. Hercules hunted it up hill and down dale for a whole year, and when at last he caught it, he got into trouble with Apollo and Diana about it, and had hard work to appease them; but he did so at last; and for his fourth labour was sent to catch alive a horrid wild boar on Mount Erymanthus. He followed the beast through a deep swamp, caught it in a net, and brought it to Mycenæ.

The fifth task was a curious one. Augeas, king of Elis, had immense herds, and kept his stables and cow-houses in a frightful state of filth, and Eurystheus, hoping either to disgust Hercules or kill him by the unwholesomeness of the work, sent him to clean them. Hercules, without telling Augeas it was his appointed task, offered to do it if he were repaid the tenth of the herds, and received the promise on oath. Then he dug a canal, and turned the water of two rivers into the stables, so as effectually to cleanse them; but when Augeas heard it was his task, he tried to cheat him of the payment, and on the other hand Eurystheus said, as he had been rewarded, it could not count as one of his labours, and ordered him off to clear the woods near Lake Stymphalis of some horrible birds, with brazen beaks and claws, and ready-made arrows for feathers, which ate human flesh. To get them to rise out of the forest was his first difficulty, but Pallas lent him a brazen clapper, which made them take to their wings; then he shot them with his poisoned arrows, killed many, and drove the rest away.

King Minos of Crete had once vowed to sacrifice to the gods whatever should appear from the sea. A beautiful white bull came, so fine that it tempted him not to keep his word, and he was punished by the bull going mad, and doing all sorts of damage in Crete; so that Eurystheus thought it would serve as a labour for Hercules to bring the animal to Mycenæ. In due time back came the hero, with the bull, quite subdued, upon his shoulders; and, having shown it, he let it loose again to run about Greece.

He had a harder task in getting the mares of the Thracian king, Diomêdes, which were fed on man's flesh. He overcame their grooms, and drove the beasts away; but he was overtaken by Diomêdes, and, while fighting with him and his people, put the mares under the charge of a friend; but when the battle was over, and Diomêdes killed, he found that they had eaten up their keeper. However, when he had fed them on the dead body of their late master, they grew mild and manageable, and he brought them home.

The next expedition was against the Amazons, a nation of women warriors, who lived somewhere on the banks of the Euxine or Black Sea, kept their husbands in subjection, and seldom brought up a son. The bravest of all the Amazons was the queen, Hippolyta, to whom Mars had given a belt as a reward for her valour. Eurystheus' daughter wanted this belt, and Hercules was sent to fetch it. He was so hearty, honest, and good-natured, that he talked over Hippolyta, and she promised him her girdle; but Juno, to make mischief, took the form of an Amazon, and persuaded the ladies that their queen was being deluded and stolen away by a strange man, so they mounted their horses and came down to rescue her. He thought she had been treacherous, and there was a great fight, in which he killed her, and carried off her girdle.

Far out in the west, near the ocean flowing round the world, were herds of purple oxen, guarded by a two-headed dog, and belonging to a giant with three bodies called Geryon, who lived in the isle of Erythria, in the outmost ocean. Passing Lybia, Hercules came to the end of the Mediterranean Sea, Neptune's domain, and there set up two pillars — namely, Mounts Calpe and Abyla — on each side a the Straits of Gibraltar. The rays of the sun scorched him, and in wrath he shot at it with his arrows, when Helios, instead of being angry, admired his boldness, and gave him his golden cup, wherewith to cross the outer ocean, which he did safely, although old Oceanus, who was king there, put up his hoary head, and tried to frighten him by shaking the bowl. It was large enough to hold all the herd of oxen, when Hercules had killed dog, herdsman, and giant, and he returned it safely to Helios when he had crossed the ocean. The oxen were sacrificed to Juno, Eurystheus' friend.

Again Eurystheus sent Hercules to the utmost parts of the earth. This time it was to bring home the golden apples which grew in the gardens of the Hesperides, the daughters of old Atlas, who dwelt in the land of Hesperus the Evening Star, and, together with a dragon, guarded the golden tree in a beautiful garden. Hercules made a long journey, apparently round by the North, and on his way had to wrestle with a dreadful giant named Antæus. Though thrown down over and over again, Antæus rose up twice as strong every time, till Hercules found out that he grew in force whenever he touched his mother earth, and therefore, lifting him up in those mightiest of arms, the hero squeezed the breath out of him. By-and-by he came to Mount Caucasus, where he found the chained Prometheus, and, aiming an arrow at the eagle, killed the tormentor, and set the Titan free. In return, Prometheus gave him much good counsel, and indeed seems to have gone with him to Atlas, who, according to this story, was still able to move, in spite of the petrifaction by Hercules' grandfather. Atlas undertook to go to his daughters, and get the apples, if Hercules would hold up the skies for him in the meantime. Hercules agreed, and Atlas shifted the heavens to his shoulders, went, and presently returned with three apples of gold, but said he would take them to Eurystheus, and Hercules must continue to bear the load of the skies. Prometheus bade Hercules say he could not hold them without a pad for them to rest on his head. Atlas took them again to hold while the pad was put on; and thereupon Hercules picked up the apples, and left the old giant to his load.

One more labour remained — namely, to bring up the three-headed watch-dog, Cerberus, from the doors of Tartarus. Mercury and Pallas both came to attend him, and led him alive among the shades, who all fled from him, except Medusa and one brave youth. He gave them the blood of an ox to drink, and made his way to Pluto's throne, where he asked leave to take Cerberus to the upper world with him. Pluto said he might, if he could overcome Cerberus without weapons; and this he did, struggling with the dog, with no protection but the lion's skin, and dragging him up to the light, where the foam that fell from the jaws of one of the three mouths produced the plant called aconite, or hellebore, which is dark and poisonous. After showing the beast to Eurystheus, Hercules safely returned him to the underworld, and thus completed his twelve great labours.

## CHAP. VI. — THE ARGONAUTS.

You remember that Cadmus founded Thebes. One of his daughters was named Ino. She married a son of King Æolus, who had been married before, and had two children, Phryxus and Helle. Ino was a cruel stepmother, and deceived her husband into thinking that the oracle at Delphi required him to sacrifice his son to Jupiter; but as the poor boy stood before the altar, down from the skies came a ram with a golden fleece, which took both the children on his back, and flew away with them over land and sea; but poor Helle let go in passing the narrow strait between Asia and Europe, fell into the sea, and was drowned. The strait was called after her, the Hellespont, or Helle's Sea. Phryxus came safely to Colchis, on the Black Sea, and was kindly received by Æetes, the king of the country. They sacrificed the golden-woolled ram to Jupiter, and nailed up its fleece to a tree in the grove of Mars.

Some time after, Pelias, the usurping king of Iolcus, was driving a mule-car through the market-place, when he saw a fine young man, with hair flowing on his shoulders, two spears in his hand, and only one sandal. He was very much afraid, for it had been foretold to him by an oracle that he would be slain by the man with one foot bare. And this youth was really Jason, the son of his brother Æson, from whom he had taken the kingdom. Fearing that he would kill the child, Æson had sent it away to the cave of the Centaur Chiron, by whom Jason had been bred up, and had now come to seek his fortune. He had lost his shoe in the mud, while kindly carrying an old woman across a river, little knowing that she was really the goddess Juno, who had come down in that form to make trial of the kindness of men, and who was thus made his friend for ever. Pelias sent for the young stranger the next day, and asked him what he would do if he knew who was the man fated to kill him. "I should send him to fetch the Golden Fleece," said Jason.

"Then go and fetch it," said Pelias.

Jason thereupon began building a ship, which he called Argo, and proclaimed the intended expedition throughout Greece, thus gathering together all the most famous heroes then living, most of whom had, like him, been brought up by the great Centaur Chiron. Hercules was one of them, and another was Theseus, the great hero of the Ionian city of Athens, whose prowess was almost equal to that of Hercules. He had caught and killed the great white bull which Hercules had brought from Crete and let loose, and he had also destroyed the horrid robber Procrustes (the Stretcher), who had kept two iron bedsteads, one long and one short. He put tall men into the short bed, and cut them down to fit it, and short men into the long bed, pulling them out till they died, until Theseus finished his life on one of his own beds.

BUILDING THE ARGO.

Another deed of Theseus was in Crete. The great white bull which Minos ought to have sacrificed had left a horrible offspring, a monster called the Minotaur, half man and half bull, which ate human flesh, and did horrible harm, till a clever artificer named Dædalus made a dwelling for it called the Labyrinth, approached by so many cross paths, winding in and out in a maze, that everyone who entered it was sure to lose himself; and the Minotaur could never get out, but still they fed him there; and as Athens was subject to Crete, the people were required to send every year a tribute of seven youths and seven maidens for the Minotaur to devour. Theseus offered himself to be one of these, telling his father that whereas a black sail was always carried by the ship that bore these victims to their death, he would, if he succeeded in killing the Minotaur, as he hoped to do, hoist a white one when coming home. When he reached Crete, he won the heart of Minos' daughter Ariadne, who gave him a skein of thread: by unwinding this as he went he would leave a clue behind him, by which he could find his way out of the labyrinth, after killing the monster. When this was done, by his great skill and strength, he took ship again, and Ariadne came with him; but he grew tired of her, and left her behind in the isle of Naxos, where Bacchus found her weeping, consoled her, and gave her a starry crown, which may be seen in the sky on a summer night. Theseus, meantime, went back to Athens, but he had forgotten his promise about the white sail, and his poor old father, seeing the black one, as he sat watching on the rocks, thought that ill news was coming, fell down, and was drowned, just as Theseus sailed safely into port. Theseus was a friend of Hercules, had been with him on his journey to the land of the Amazons, and had married one of them named Antiope.

Two more of the Argonauts were Castor and Pollux, the twin sons of Leda, queen of Sparta. She had also two daughters, named Helen and Clytemnestra, and Helen was growing into the most beautiful woman in the world. These children, in the fable, had been hatched from two huge swans' eggs; Castor and Clytemnestra were in one egg, and Pollux and Helen in the other. Castor and Pollux were the most loving of brothers, and while Castor was famous for horsemanship, Pollux was the best of boxers. They, too, had been pupils of Chiron; so was Peleus of Ægina, who had wooed Thetis, one of the fifty Nereids, or sea-nymphs, though she changed herself into all sorts of forms when he caught her first — fire, water, a serpent, and a lioness; but he held her fast through all, and at last she listened to him, and all the gods and goddesses had come to the wedding feast. They had one son, named Achilles, whom Thetis had tried to make immortal after Ceres' fashion, by putting him on the fire at night; but, like Triptolemus' mother, Peleus had cried out and spoilt the spell. Then she took the boy to the river Styx, and bathed him there, so that he became invulnerable all over, except in the heel by which she held him. The child was now in Chiron's cave, being fed with the marrow of lions and bears, to make him strong and brave.

One more Argonaut must be mentioned, namely, the minstrel Orpheus. He was the son of the muse Calliope, and was looked on as the first of the many glorious singers of Greece, who taught the noblest and best lessons. His music, when he played on the lyre, was so sweet, that all the animals, both fierce and gentle, came round to hear it; and not only these, but even the trees and rocks gathered round, entranced by the sweetness.

All these and more, to the number of fifty, joined Jason in his enterprise. The Argo, the ship which bore them, had fifty oars, and in the keel was a piece of wood from the great oak of Dodona, which could speak for the oracles. When all was ready, Jason stood on the poop, and poured forth a libation from a golden cup, praying aloud to Jupiter, to the Winds, the Days, the Nights, and to Fate to grant them a favourable voyage. Old Chiron came down from his hills to cheer them, and pray for their return; and as the oars kept measured time, Orpheus struck his lyre in tune with their splash in the blue waters.

They had many adventures. After passing the Hellespont, they found in the Propontis, which we call the Sea of Marmora, an islet called the Bears' Hill, inhabited by giants with six arms, whom they slew.

In Mysia a youth named Hylas went ashore to fetch water, but was caught by the nymphs of the stream and taken captive. Hercules, hearing his cry, went in search of him, and, as neither returned, the Argo sailed without them. No more was heard of Hylas, but Hercules went back to Argos.

They next visited Phineus, a wise old blind king, who was tormented by horrid birds called Harpies, with women's faces. These monsters always came down when he was going to eat, devoured the food, and spoilt what they did not eat. The Argonauts having among them two winged sons of Boreas (the north wind), hunted these horrible creatures far out into the Mediterranean. Phineus then told them that they would have to pass between some floating rocks called the Symplegades, which were always enveloped in mist, were often driven together by the wind, and crushed whatever was between. He told them to let fly a dove, and if it went through safely they might follow. They did so, and the dove came out at the other side, but with her tail clipped off as the rocks met. However, on went the Argo, each hero rowing for his life, and Juno and Pallas helping them; and, after all, they were but just in time, and lost the ornaments at their stern!

Fate had decreed that, when once a ship passed through these rocks unhurt, they should become fixed, and thus they were no longer dangerous. It does not seem unlikely that this story might have come from some report of the dangers of icebergs. Of course there are none in the Black Sea, but the Greeks, who knew little beyond their own shores, seem to have fancied that this was open to the north into the great surrounding ocean, and the Phœnicians, who were much more adventurous sailors than they, may have brought home histories of the perils they met in the Atlantic Ocean.

The Argonauts had one more encounter with Hercules' old foes, the birds of Stymphalis, and after this safely arrived at Colchis, and sailed into the mouth of the river Phasis, from which it is said the pheasant takes its name.

## CHAP. VII. — THE SUCCESS OF THE ARGONAUTS.

When Jason arrived at Colchis, he sent to King Æetes, and asked of him the Golden Fleece. To this Æetes replied that he might have it, provided he could yoke the two brazen-footed bulls with flaming breath, which had been a present from Vulcan, and with them plough a piece of land, and sow it with the dragon's teeth. Pallas had given Æetes half the teeth of the dragon of Thebes, which had been slain by Cadmus.

The task seemed beyond his reach, till Medea, the wicked witch, daughter of Æetes, promised to help him, on condition that he would marry her, and take her to Greece. When Jason had sworn to do so, Medea gave him an ointment with which to rub himself, also his shield and spear. For a whole day afterwards neither sword nor fire should hurt him, and he would thus be able to master the bulls. So he found it; he made them draw the plough, and then he sowed the teeth, which came up, like those sown by Cadmus, as armed men, who began to attack him; but, as Medea had bidden him, he threw a stone among them, and they began to fight with one another, so that he could easily kill the few who spared each other.

Still Æetes refused to give him the fleece, and was about to set fire to the Argo, and kill the crew; but Medea warned Jason in time, and led him to the spot where it was nailed against a tree. Orpheus lulled the guardian dragon to sleep with his lyre, while Jason took down the fleece; and Medea joined them, carrying in her arms her little brother, whom she had snatched from his bed with a cruel purpose, for when her father took alarm and gave chase, she cut the poor child to pieces, and strewed his limbs on the stream of the Phasis, so that, while her father waited to collect them, the Argo had time to sail away.

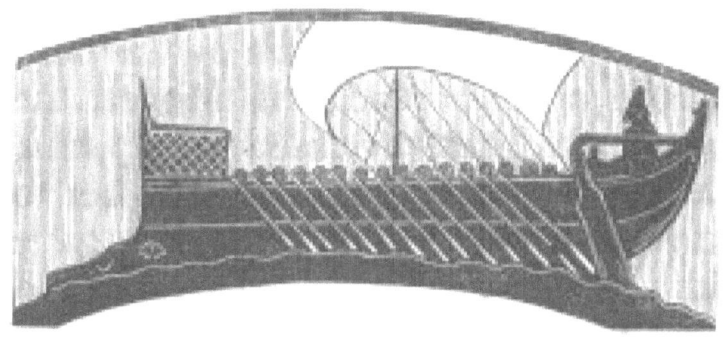

It did not return by the same route, but went to the north, and came to the isle of the goddess Circe, who purified Jason and Medea from the blood of the poor boy. Then they came to the isle of the Sirens, creatures like fair maidens, who stood on the shore singing so sweetly that no sailor could resist the charm; but the moment any man reached the shore, they strangled him and sucked his blood. Warned by Medea, Orpheus played and sang so grandly as to drown their fatal song, and the Argo came out into the Mediterranean somewhere near Trinacria, the three-cornered island now called Sicily, where they had to pass between two lofty cliffs. In a cave under one of these lived a monster called Scylla, with twelve limbs and six long necks, with a dog's head to each, ready each to seize a man out of every ship that passed; but it was safer to keep on her side than to go to the other cliff, for there a water-witch named Charybdis lived in a whirlpool, and was sure to suck the whole ship in, and swallow it up. However, for her husband Peleus' sake, Thetis and her sister Nereids came and guided the Argo safely through.

When the crew returned to Iolcus, they had only been absent four months; and Jason gave the fleece to his uncle Pelias, and dedicated the Argo to Neptune. He found his father Æson grown very old, but Medea undertook to restore him to youth. She went forth by moonlight, gathered a number of herbs, and then, putting them in a caldron, she cut old Æson into pieces, threw them in, and boiled them all night. In the morning Æson appeared as a lively black-haired young man, no older than his son. Pelias' daughters came and begged her to teach them the same spell. She feigned to do so, but she did not tell them the true herbs, and thus the poor maidens only slew their father, and did not bring him to life again. The son of Pelias drove the treacherous Medea and her husband from Iolcus, and they went to Corinth, where they lived ten years, until Jason grew weary of Medea, and put her away, in order to marry Creusa, the king's daughter. In her rage, Medea sent the bride the fatal gift of a poisoned robe, then she killed her own children, and flew away, in a chariot drawn by winged serpents, to the east, where she became the mother of a son named Medus, from whom the nation of Medes was descended. As to Jason, he had fallen asleep at noon one hot day under the shade of the Argo, where it was drawn up on the sand by Neptune's temple, when a bit of wood broke off from the prow, fell on his head, and killed him.

CORINTH.

Of the other Argonauts, Orpheus went to Thessaly, and there taught and softened the people much by his music. He married a fair maiden named Eurydice, with whom he lived happily and peacefully, till she was bitten by a venomous serpent and died. Orpheus was so wretched that he set forth to try to bring her back from Tartarus. He went with nothing but his lyre, and his music was so sweet that Cerberus stood listening, and let him pass, and all the torments of the

Danaids, Sisyphus and all the rest, ceased while he was playing. His song even brought tears into Pluto's eyes, and Proserpine, who guarded the female dead, gave him leave to take back Eurydice to the light of day, provided he did not once look back as he led her out of Tartarus.

Orpheus had to walk first, and, as he went up the long, dark cavern, with Eurydice behind him, he carefully obeyed, till, just as he was reaching the upper air, he unhappily forgot, and turned his head to see whether she were following. He just saw her stretch out her hands to him, and then she was drawn back, and vanished from his sight. The gates were closed, and he had lost her again. After this he wandered sadly about, all his songs turned to woe, until at last the Bacchanal women, in fury at his despising the foul rites of their god, tore him limb from limb. The Muses collected his remains, and gave them funeral rites, and Jupiter placed his lyre in the skies, where you may know it by one of the brightest of all our stars.

Hercules also made another visit to the realms below. Admetus, one of the Æolian kings, had obtained from Apollo that, when the time came for him to die, his life should be prolonged if anyone would submit to death in his turn. The call came while Admetus was still young, and he besought his old father, and then his mother, to die in his stead; but they would not, and it was his fair young wife Alcestis who gave her life for his. Just as she was laid in the tomb, Hercules came to visit Admetus, and, on hearing what had happened, he went down to the kingdom of Pluto and brought her back. Or some say he sat by her tomb, and wrestled with Death when he came to seize her.

But, strong as he was, Hercules had in time to meet death himself. He had married a nymph named Deianira, and was taking her home, when he came to a river where a Centaur named Nessus lived, and gained his bread by carrying travellers over on his back. Hercules paid him the price for carrying Deianira over, while he himself crossed on foot; but as soon as the river was between them, the faithless Centaur began to gallop away with the lady. Hercules sent an arrow after him, which brought him to the ground, and as he was dying he prepared his revenge, by telling Deianira that his blood was enchanted with love for her, and that if ever she found her husband's affection failing her, she had only to make him put on a garment anointed with it, and his heart would return to her: he knew full well that his blood was full of the poison of the Hydra, but poor Deianira believed him, and had saved some of the blood before Hercules came up.

Several years after, Hercules made prisoner a maiden named Iole, in Lydia, after gaining a great victory. Landing in the island of Eubœa, he was going to make a great sacrifice to Jupiter, and sent home to Deianira for a festal garment to wear at it. She was afraid he was falling in love with Iole, and steeped the garment in the preparation she had made from Nessus' blood. No sooner did Hercules put it on, than his veins were filled with agony, which nothing could assuage. He tried to tear off the robe, but the skin and flesh came with it, and his blood was poisoned beyond relief. He sailed home, and when Deianira saw the state he was in she hung herself for grief, while he charged Hylas, his eldest son, to take care of Iole, and marry her as soon as he grew up. Then, unable to bear the pain any longer, and knowing that by his twelve tasks he had earned the prize of endless life, he went to Mount Œta, crying aloud with the pain, so that the rocks rang again with the sound. He gave his quiver of arrows to his friend Philoctetes, charging him to collect his ashes and bury them, but never to make known the spot; and then he tore up, with his mighty strength, trees by the roots enough to form a funeral pile, lay down on it, and called on his friend to set fire to it; but no one could bear to do so, till a shepherd consented to thrust in a torch. Then thunder was heard, a cloud came down, and he was borne away to Olympus, while Philoctetes collected and buried the ashes.

His young sons were banished by Eurystheus, and were taken by his old friend Iolaus to seek shelter in various cities, but only the Athenians were brave enough to let them remain. Theseus had been driven away and banished from Athens; but the citizens sheltered the sons of the hero, and, when Eurystheus pursued them, a battle was fought on the isthmus of Corinth, in which the old enemy of Hercules was killed by Iolaus, with all his sons. Then the Heraclieds (sons of Hercules) were going to fight their way back to Argos, but an army met them at the isthmus, and was going to give them battle, when Hylas proposed that he should fight with a single champion chosen on the other side. If he gained, he was to be restored to the kingdom of Perseus; if not, there was to be a truce for a hundred years. Hylas had not the strength of his father; he was slain, and his brothers had to retreat and bide their time.

Argos came into the power of Agamemnon, who had married Clytemnestra, the sister of Castor and Pollux, while his brother Menelaus married the beautiful Helen. All the Greek heroes had been suitors for Helen, the fairest woman living, and they all swore to one another that, choose she whom she might, they would all stand by him, and punish anyone who might try to steal her from him. Her choice fell on Menelaus, and soon after her wedding her brother Castor was slain, and though Pollux was immortal, he could not bear to live without his brother, and prayed to share his death; upon which Jupiter made them both stars, the bright ones called Gemini, or the Twins, and Menelaus reigned with Helen at Sparta, as Agamemnon did at Mycenæ.

These two were sons of Atreus, and were descended from Tantalus, once a favourite of the gods, who used to come down and feast with him, until once he took his son Pelops and dressed him for their meal. Jupiter found it out, collected the limbs, and restored the boy to life; but Ceres had been so distracted with grief about her daughter, that she had eaten one shoulder, and Jupiter gave him an ivory one instead. Tantalus was sent to Tartarus, where his punishment was to pine with hunger and thirst, with a feast before him, where he neither could touch the food nor the drink, because there was a rock hung over his head threatening to crush him. Pelops was a wonderful charioteer, and won his bride in the chariot race, having bribed the charioteer of his rival to leave out the linchpins of his wheels. Afterwards, when the charioteer asked a reward, Pelops threw him into the sea; and this was the second crime that brought a doom on the race. Pelops gave his name to the whole peninsula now called the Morea, or mulberry-leaf, but which was all through ancient times known as the Peloponnesus, or Isle of Pelops. He reigned at Elis, and after his death his sons Atreus and Thyestes struggled for the rule, but both were horribly wicked men, and Atreus was said to have killed two sons of Thyestes, and served them up to him at a feast. There was, therefore, a heavy curse on the whole family, both on Ægisthus, son of Thyestes, and on his cousins Agamemnon and Menelaus, the Atridæ, or sons of Atreus.

## CHAP. VIII. – THE CHOICE OF PARIS.

The gods and goddesses were merrily feasting when Ate, the goddess of strife, desirous of making mischief, threw down among them a golden apple, engraven with the words, "This apple to the Fair." The three goddesses, Juno, Pallas, and Venus, each thought it meant for her – one having the beauty of dignity, the other the beauty of wisdom, and the third the beauty of grace and fairness. They would not accept the award of any of the gods, lest they should not be impartial; but they declared that no one should decide between them but Paris, a shepherd, though a king's son, who was keeping his flocks on Mount Ida.

Each goddess tried to allure him to choose her by promises. Juno offered him a mighty throne; Pallas promised to make him the wisest of men; Venus declared that she would give him the fairest woman on earth for his wife for ten years – she could assure him of no more. And it was Venus to whom Paris assigned the golden apple of discord, thus bitterly offending Juno and Pallas, who became the enemies of his nation.

PLAINS OF TROY.

His nation was the Trojan, who dwelt on the east coast of the Ægean Sea, and were of the Pelasgic race. Their chief city was Troy, with the citadel Ilium, lying near the banks of the rivers Simois and Scamander, between the sea shore and the wooded mount of Ida, in the north-east of the peninsula we call Asia Minor. The story went that the walls had been built by Neptune and Apollo, the last of whom had brought the stones to their place by the music of his lyre; but the king who was then reigning had refused to pay them, and had thus made them also his foes. But within the citadel was an image of Pallas, three ells long, with a spear in one hand and a distaff in the other, which was called the Palladium. It was said to have been given by Jupiter to Ilus, the first founder of the city; and as long as it was within the walls, the place could never be taken.

The present king was Priam, and his wife was Hecuba. They had nineteen children, and lived in a palace built round a court, with an altar in the middle, their sons having houses likewise opening into the court. Paris, who was worthless and pleasure-loving, was the eldest son; Hector, a very noble person, was the second. After Paris had given judgment in her favour, Venus directed him to build a ship, and go to visit the Greek kings. He was kindly entertained everywhere, and especially at Sparta; and here it was that Venus fulfilled her promise, by helping him to steal away Helen, the fairest of women, while her husband Menelaus was gone to Crete.

As soon as Menelaus found out how his hospitality had been misused, he called upon all the Greek heroes to remember their oath, and help him to recover his wife, and take vengeance on Paris. Everyone replied to the call; but the wise Ulysses, grandson of Sisyphus, and king of the little isle of Ithaca, could not bear to leave his home, or his fair young wife Penelope, for a war which he knew would be long and terrible, so he feigned to be mad, and began furiously ploughing the sea shore with a yoke of oxen. However, the next cleverest hero, Palamedes, to prove him, placed his infant son Telemachus full in the way of the plough, and when Ulysses turned it aside from the child, they declared that his madness was only pretended, and he was forced to go with them.

The Nereid Thetis knew that if her brave and beautiful son Achilles went to Troy, he would die there; so she dressed him as a maiden, and placed him at the court of the king of Scyros, where he stayed for love of one of the king's daughters. But the Greeks had a man named Calchas, who was an augur — that is, he could tell what was going to happen by the flight of birds, by the clouds, and by the inwards of sacrificed animals. Calchas told the Greeks that Troy would never be taken unless Achilles went with them. So Ulysses, guessing where the youth was, disguised himself as a merchant, and went with his wares to the palace of Scyros. All the maidens came forth to look at them, and while most were busy with the jewels and robes, one, tall and golden-haired, seemed to care for nothing but a bright sword, holding it with a strong, firm hand. Then Ulysses knew he had found Achilles, and told him of the famous war that was beginning, and the youth threw off his maiden's garb, put on his armour, and went eagerly with them; but before he went he married the fair Deidamia, and left her to wait for him at Scyros, where she had a son named Pyrrhus.

Indeed the Greeks were whole years gathering their forces, and when they did all meet at last, with their ships and men, Agamemnon, king of Mycenæ, Menelaus' brother, took the lead of them all. As they were sacrificing to Jupiter, a snake glided up a tree, where there was a sparrow's nest, and ate up all the eight young ones, and then the mother bird. On seeing this, Calchas foretold that the war would last nine years, and after the ninth Troy would be taken.

However, they sailed on, till at Aulis they were stopped by foul winds for many days, and Calchas told them it was because of Agamemnon's broken vow. He had sworn, one year, to sacrifice to Diana the fairest thing that was born in his house or lands. The fairest thing that was born was his little daughter Iphigenia; but he could not bear to sacrifice her, and so had tried offering his choicest kid. Now Diana sent these winds to punish him, and the other kings required him to give up his child. So a message was sent to her mother, Clytemnestra, to send her, on pretence that she was to be married to Achilles, and when she came to Aulis she found that it was only to be offered up. However, she resigned herself bravely, and was ready to die for her father and the cause; but just as Agamemnon had his sword ready, and had covered her face that he might not see her pleading eyes as he was slaying her, Diana took pity, darted down in a cloud, and in the place of the maiden a white hind lay on the altar to be offered. Iphigenia was really carried off to serve as priestess at Diana's temple at Tauris, but it was long before it was known what had become of her, and Clytemnestra never forgave Agamemnon for what he had intended to do.

At the isle of Tenedos the Greeks had to leave behind Philoctetes, the friend of Hercules, who had his quiver of poisoned arrows, because the poor man had a wound in his heel, which was in such a dreadful state that no one could bear to come near him. One story was that he was bitten by a water-snake, another that when he was just setting off he had been over-persuaded to show where he had buried the ashes of Hercules. He did not say one word, but stamped with his foot on the place, and an arrow fell out at the moment and pierced his heel. At any rate, he and the arrows were left behind, while the Greeks reached the coast of Troy.

GREEK SHIPS.

The augurs had declared that the first man who touched the shore would be the first to be killed. Achilles threw his shield before him, and leaped out of the ship upon that; but Protesilaus leaped without so doing, and was slain almost instantly by the Trojans. When his wife Laodamia heard of his death, she grieved and pined so piteously that his spirit could not rest, and Mercury gave him leave to come back and spend three hours with her on earth. He came, but when she tried to embrace him she found that he was only thin air, which could not be grasped, and when the time was over he vanished from her sight. Then Laodamia made an image of him, and treated it as a god; and when her father forbade her to do this, she leaped into the fire, and thus perished.

The chief of the Greeks were Agamemnon, king of Mycenæ, his brother Menelaus of Sparta, and Achilles of Ægina, whose men were called Myrmidons, and said to be descended from ants. His friend, to whom he was devoted, was called Patroclus. He was the most perfect warrior in the army, but Diomed the Ætolian came near him in daring, and Ajax of Salamis, son of Telamon, was the biggest and strongest man. His brother Teucer used to stand behind his shield and aim arrows at the Trojans. There was another Ajax, from Locria, called after his father Oileus. The oldest man in the camp was Nestor, king of Pylos, who had been among the Argonauts, and had been a friend of Hercules, and was much looked up to. The wisest men were Ulysses of Ithaca, and Palamedes, who is said to have invented the game of chess to amuse the warriors in the camp; but Ulysses never forgave Palamedes for his trick on the shore at Ithaca, and managed to make him be suspected of secret dealings with the Trojans, and put to death. Each of these brought a band of fighting men, and they had their ships, which were not much more than large boats, drawn up high and dry on the shore behind the camp. They fought with swords and spears, which latter were thrown with the hand. Some had bows and arrows, and the chiefs generally went to battle in a chariot, an open car drawn by two horses, and driven by some trusty friend, who held the horses while the chief stood up and launched spear after spear among the enemy. There was no notion of mercy to the fallen; prisoners were seldom made, and if a man was once down, unless his friends could save him, he was sure to be killed.

During the first eight years of the war we do not hear much of the Greeks. They seem to have been taking and wasting the cities belonging to the Trojans all round the country. The home of Andromache, Hector's good and loving wife, was destroyed, and her parents and brothers killed; and Priam's cousin Æneas was also driven in from Mount Ida, with his old father Anchises, and wife and little son. In the ninth year of the war the Greeks drew up their forces round the walls of Troy itself, their last exploit having been the taking of the city of Chrysæ, where they had gained a great deal of plunder. All captives were then made slaves, and in the division of the spoil a maiden named Briseis was given to Achilles, while Agamemnon took one called Chryseis, the daughter of Chryses, priest of Apollo.

## CHAP. IX. — THE SIEGE OF TROY.

We have come to the part of this siege which is told us in the Iliad, the oldest poem we know, except the Psalms, and one of the very finest. It begins by telling how Chryses prayed to Apollo to help him to get back his daughter, and Apollo sent a plague upon the Greeks in their camp. Calchas told them it was because of Chryseis, and they forced Agamemnon to give her safely back to her father. His pride, however, was hurt, and he said he must have Briseis in her stead, and sent and took her from Achilles. In his wrath Achilles declared he would not fight any more for the Greeks, and his mother Thetis begged Jupiter to withdraw his aid from them likewise, that they might feel the difference.

The Trojans went out to attack them, and when they were drawn up in battle array, old Priam made Helen come and sit by him on the battlements over the gateway, to tell him who all the chiefs were. It was proposed that, instead of causing the death of numbers who had nothing to do with the quarrel, Menelaus and Paris should fight hand-to-hand for Helen; and they began; but as soon as Venus saw that her favourite Paris was in danger, she came in a cloud, snatched him away, and set him down in Helen's chamber, where his brother Hector found him reclining at his ease, on coming to upbraid him for keeping out of the battle, where so many better men than he were dying for his crime. Very different were Hector's ways. He parted most tenderly with his wife Andromache, and his little son Astyanax, who was so young that he clung crying to his nurse, afraid of his father's tall helmet and horsehair crest. Hector took the helmet off before he lifted the little one in his arms and prayed to the gods for him.

Each day the Trojans gained, though one day Jupiter forbade any of the gods or goddesses to interfere, and on another he let them all go down and fight for their own parties. He was himself impartial; but one day Juno managed to borrow Venus' girdle, which made her so charming that nothing could resist her, and she lulled him to sleep. During that time the Greeks prevailed again, but this only lasted till Jupiter awoke, and then the Trojans gained great success. All the Greek heroes were disabled one after another, and Hector and his men broke through the rampart they had made round their camp, and were about to burn the ships, when Patroclus, grieved at finding all his friends wounded, came to Achilles with an entreaty that he might be allowed to send out the Myrmidons, and try to save the ships. Achilles consented, and dressed Patroclus in his own armour. Then all gave way before the fresh Myrmidons led by Patroclus, and the Trojans were chased back to their walls; but as Hector made a last stand before the gates, Apollo, who loved Troy because he had built the walls, caused a sunbeam to strike on Patroclus and make him faint, so that Hector easily struck him down and killed him. Then there was a desperate fight over his body. The Trojans did get the armour off it, but the Greeks saved the corpse, and had almost reached the rampart, when the Trojans came thicker and more furiously on them, and were almost bursting in, when Achilles, hearing the noise, came out, and, standing on the rampart just as he was, all unarmed, gave a terrible thundering shout, at which the Trojans were filled with dismay, and fled back in confusion, while the corpse of Patroclus was borne into the tent, where Achilles mourned over it, with many tears and vows of vengeance against Hector.

ACHILLES BINDING HIS ARMOUR ON PATROCLUS.

His mother Thetis came from the sea and wept with him, and thence she went to Vulcan, from whom she obtained another beautiful suit of armour, with a wondrous shield, representing Greek life in every phase of war or peace; and in this Achilles went forth again to the battle. He drove the Trojans before his irresistible might, came up with Hector, chased him round and round the walls of Troy, and at length came up with him and slew him. Then, when Patroclus had been laid on a costly funeral pile, Achilles dragged Hector's body at the back of his chariot three times round it. Further, in honour of his friend, he had games of racing in chariots and on foot, wrestling, boxing, throwing heavy stones, and splendidly rewarded those who excelled with metal tripods, weapons, and robes.

But when poor old Priam, grieving that his son's corpse should lie unburied, thus hindering his shade from being at rest, came forth at night, in disguise, to beg it from Achilles, the hero received the old man most kindly, wept at the thought of his own old father Peleus, fed and warmed him, and sent home the body of Hector most honourably.

Here ends the Iliad. It is from other poems that the rest of the history is taken, and we know that Achilles performed many more great exploits, until Paris was aided by Apollo to shoot an arrow into the heel which alone could be wounded, and thus the hero died. There was another great fight over his body, but Ajax and Ulysses rescued it at last; Ajax bore it to the ships, and Ulysses kept back the Trojans. Thetis and all the Nereids and all the Muses came to mourn over him; and when he was burnt in the funeral pile she bore away his spirit to the white island, while the Greeks raised a huge mound in his honour. She promised his armour to the Greek who had done most to rescue his corpse. The question lay between Ajax and Ulysses, and Trojan captives being appointed as judges, gave sentence in favour of Ulysses. Ajax was so grieved that he had a fit of frenzy, fancied the cattle were the Greeks who slighted him, killed whole flocks in his rage, and, when he saw what he had done, fell on his own sword and died.

SEPULCHRAL MOUND, KNOWN AS THE TOMB OF AJAX.

Having lost these great champions, the Greeks resolved to fetch Achilles' young son Pyrrhus to the camp, and also to get again those arrows of Hercules which Philoctetes had with him. Ulysses and Pyrrhus were accordingly sent to fetch him from his lonely island. They found him howling with pain, but he would not hear of coming away with them. So Ulysses stole his quiver while he was asleep, but when he awoke and missed it his lamentations so moved young Pyrrhus that he gave them back; and this so touched the heart of Philoctetes that he consented to return to the camp. There Machaon, the physician of the Greeks, healed his foot, and he soon after shot Paris with one of the arrows.

Instead of now giving up Helen, Deiphobus and Helenus, the two next brothers, quarrelled as to which should marry her, and when she was given to Deiphobus, Helenus was so angry that he went out and wandered in the forests of Mount Ida, where he was made prisoner by Ulysses, who contrived to find out from him that Troy could never be taken while it had the Palladium within it. Accordingly, Ulysses and Diomed set out, and, climbing over the wall by night, stole the wondrous image. While the Trojans were dismayed at the loss, the Greeks seemed to have changed their minds. They took ship and went away, and all the surviving Trojans, relieved from their siege, rushed down to the shore, where all they found was a monstrous wooden horse. While they were looking at it in wonder, a Greek came out of the rocks, and told them that his name was Sinon, and that he had been cruelly left behind by the Greeks, who had grown weary of the siege and gone home, but that if the wonderful horse were once taken into Troy it would serve as another Palladium.

The priest of Neptune, Laocöon, did not believe the story, and declared that Sinon was a spy; but he was cut short in his remonstrance by two huge serpents, which glided out of the sea and devoured him and his two sons. Cassandra, too, a daughter of Priam, who had the gift of prophecy, but was fated never to be believed, shrieked with despair when she saw the Trojans harnessing themselves to the horse to drag it into Troy, but nobody heeded her, and there was a great feast to dedicate it to Pallas. Helen perhaps guessed or knew what it meant, for at dark she walked round it, and called the names of Ulysses, and many other Greeks, in the voices of Penelope and the other wives at home.

LAOCOÖN.

For indeed the horse was full of Greeks; and at dark Sinon lighted a beacon as a signal to the rest, who were only waiting behind the little isle of Tenedos. Then he let the others out of the horse, and slaughter and fire reigned throughout Troy. Menelaus slew Deiphobus as he tried to rise from bed, and carried Helen down to his ship. Poor old Priam tried to put on his armour and defend Hecuba and his daughters, but Pyrrhus killed him at the altar in his palace-court; and Æneas, after seeing this, and that all was lost, hurried back to his own house, took his father Anchises on his back, and his little son Iulus in one hand, his household gods in the other, and, with his wife Creusa following, tried to escape from the burning city with his own troop of warriors. All succeeded except poor Creusa, who was lost in the throng of terrified fugitives, and was never found again; but Æneas found ships on the coast, and sailed safely away to Italy.

All the rest of the Trojans were killed or made slaves. Ulysses killed Hector's poor little son, and Andromache became slave to young Pyrrhus. Cassandra clung to Pallas' statue, and Ajax Oileus, trying to drag her away, moved the statue itself — such an act of sacrilege that the Greeks had nearly stoned him on the spot — and Cassandra was given to Agamemnon. Polyxena, the youngest sister, was sacrificed on the tomb of Achilles, and poor old Hecuba went mad with grief.

FUNERAL FEAST.

## CHAP. X. — THE WANDERINGS OF ULYSSES.

The overthrow of the temples at Troy was heavily visited on the Greeks by the gods, and the disasters that befel Ulysses are the subject of another grand Greek poem called the Odyssey, from his right Greek name Odysseus. He was the special favourite of Pallas Athene, but she could not save him from many dangers. He had twelve ships, with which he set out to return to Ithaca; but as he was doubling Cape Malea, one of the rugged points of the Peloponnesus, a great storm caught him, and drove him nine days westward, till he came to an island, where he sent three men to explore, but they did not return, and he found that this was the land of the lotus-eaters, a people who always lie about in a dreamy state of repose, and that to taste the food drives away all remembrance of home and friends. He was obliged to drag his men away by force, and bind them to the benches. The lotus bean, or jujube, is really eaten in Africa, but not with these effects.

Next they came to another island, where there was a bay with rocks around, with goats leaping on them. Here Ulysses left eleven ships, and sailed with one to explore the little islet opposite. Landing with his men, he entered an enormous cavern, well stored with bowls of milk and cream, and with rows of cheeses standing on the ledges of rock. While the Greeks were regaling themselves, a noise was heard, and great flocks of sheep and goats came bleating in. Behind them came a giant, with a fir tree for a staff, and only one eye in the middle of his forehead. He was Polyphemus, one of the Cyclops, sons of Neptune, and workmen of Vulcan. He asked fiercely who the strangers were, and Ulysses told him that they were shipwrecked sailors, imploring him for hospitality in the name of the gods. Polyphemus laughed at this, saying he was stronger than the gods, and did not care for them; and, dashing two unhappy Greeks on the floor, he ate them up at once; after which he closed up the front of the cave with a monstrous rock, penned up the kids and lambs, and began to milk his goats, drank up a great quantity of milk, and fell asleep on the ground. Ulysses thought of killing him at once, but recollected that the stone at the mouth of the cave would keep him captive if the giant's strength did not move it, and abstained. In the morning the Cyclops let out his flocks, and then shut the Greeks in with the stone; but he left his staff behind, and Ulysses hardened the top of this in the fire. A skin of wine had been brought from the ships, and when Polyphemus came home in the evening, and had devoured two more Greeks, Ulysses offered it to him. It was the first wine he had tasted, and he was in raptures with it, asking his guest's name as he pledged him. "No-man," replied Ulysses, begging again for mercy. "This will I grant," said the Cyclops, "in return for thy gift. No-man shall be the last whom I devour." He drank up the whole skin of wine, and went to sleep. Then Ulysses and four of his companions seized the staff, and forced its sharpened top into the Cyclops' single eye, so that he awoke blind, and roaring with pain so loud that all the other Cyclops awoke, and came calling to know who had hurt him. "No-man," shouted back Polyphemus; and they, thinking it was only some sudden illness, went back to their caves. Meanwhile, Ulysses was fastening the remaining Greeks under the bellies of the sheep and goats, the wool and hair hanging over them. He himself clung on under the largest goat, the master of the herd. When morning came, bleatings of the herds caused the blind giant to rouse himself to roll back the stone from the entrance. He laid his hand on each beast's back, that his guests might not ride out on them, but he did not feel beneath, though he kept back Ulysses' goat for a moment caressing it, and saying, "My pretty goat, thou seest me, but I cannot see thee."

As soon as Ulysses was safe on board ship, and had thrust out from land, he called back his real name to the giant, whom he saw sitting on the stone outside his cave. Polyphemus and the other Cyclops returned by hurling rocks at the ship, but none touched it, and Ulysses reached his fleet safely. This adventure, however, had made Neptune his bitter foe, and how could he sail on Neptune's realm?

However, he next came to the Isle of the Winds, which floated about in the ocean, and was surrounded by a brazen wall. Here dwelt Æolus, with his wife and sons and daughters, and Ulysses stayed with him a whole month. At the end of it, Æolus gave Ulysses enough of each wind, tied up in separate bags, to take him safely home; but his crew fancied there was treasure in them, and while he was asleep opened all the bags at once, and the winds bursting out tossed all the ships, and then carried them back to the island, where Æolus declared that Ulysses must be a wretch forsaken of the gods, and would give him no more.

Six days later the fleet came to another cannibal island, that of the Læstrygonians, where the crews of all the ships, except that of the king himself, were caught and eaten up, and he alone escaped, and, still proceeding westward, came to another isle, belonging to Circe, the witch goddess, daughter to Helios. The comrades of Ulysses, whom he had sent to explore, did not return, and he was himself landing in search of them, when Mercury appeared to him, and warned him that, if he tasted of the bowl she would offer him, he would, like his friends, be changed by her into a hog, unless he fortified himself with the plant named moly — a white-flowered, starry sort of garlic, which Mercury gave him. Ulysses then made his way through a wood to the hall where Circe sat, waited on by four nymphs. She received him courteously, offered him her cup, and so soon as he had drunk of it she struck him with her wand, and bade him go grunt with his fellows; but as, thanks to the moly, he stood unchanged before her, he drew his sword and made her swear to do him no hurt, and to restore his companions to their proper form. They then made friends, and he stayed with her a whole year. She told him that he was fated not to return home till he had first visited the borders of the world of Pluto, and consulted Tiresias, the blind prophet. She told him what to do, and he went on beyond the Mediterranean into the outer ocean, to the land of gloom, where Helios, the sun, does not shine. Here Ulysses dug a pit, into which he poured water, wine, and the blood of a great black ram, and there flocked up to him crowds of shades, eager to drink of it, and to converse with him. All his own friends were there — Achilles, Ajax, and, to his surprise, Agamemnon — all very melancholy, and mourning for the realms of day. His mother, who had died of grief for his absence, came and blessed him; and Tiresias warned him of Neptune's anger, and of his other dangers, ere he should return to Ithaca. Terror at the ghastly troop overcame him at last, and he fled and embarked again, saw Circe once more, and found himself in the sea by which the Argo had returned. The Sirens' Isle was near, and, to prevent the perils of their song, Ulysses stopped the ears of all his crew with wax, and though he left his own open, bade them lash him to the mast, and not heed all his cries and struggles to be loosed. Thus he was the only person who ever heard the Sirens' song and lived. Scylla and Charybdis came next, and, being warned by Pallas, he thought it better to lose six than all, and so went nearest to the monster, whose six mouths at once fell on six of the crew, and tore them away.

ULYSSES TIED TO THE MAST.

The isle of Trinacria was pasture for the 360 cattle of Helios, and both Tiresias and Circe had warned Ulysses that they must not be touched. He would fain have passed it by, but his crew insisted on landing for the night, making oath not to touch the herds. At dawn such a wind arose that they could not put to sea for a month, and after eating up the stores, and living on birds and fish, they took some of the oxen when Ulysses was asleep, vowing to build a temple to Helios in recompense. They were dismayed at seeing the hides of the slain beasts creep on the ground, and at hearing their flesh low as it boiled in the cauldron. Indeed, Helios had gone to Jupiter, and threatened to stop his chariot unless he had his revenge; so as soon as the wretched crew embarked again a storm arose, the ship was struck by lightning, and Ulysses alone was saved from the wreck, floating on the mast. He came back past Scylla and Charybdis, and, clinging to the fig tree which hung over the latter, avoided being sucked into the whirlpool, and by-and-by came to land in the island of the nymph Calypso, who kept him eight years, but he pined for home all the time, and at last built a raft on which to return. Neptune was not weary of persecuting him, and raised another storm, which shattered the raft, and threw Ulysses on the island of Scheria. Here the king's fair daughter Nausicaa, going down to the stream with her maidens to wash their robes, met the shipwrecked stranger, and took him home. Her father feasted him hospitably, and sent him home in a ship, which landed him on the coast of Ithaca fast asleep, and left him there. He had been absent twenty years; and Pallas further disguised his aspect, so that he looked like a beggar, when, in order to see how matters stood, he made his way first to the hut of his trusty old swineherd Eumæus.

PORT OF ITHACA.

Nothing could be worse than things were. More than a hundred powerful young chiefs of the Ionian isles had taken possession of his palace, and were daily revelling there, thrusting his son Telemachus aside, and insisting that Penelope should choose one of them as her husband. She could only put them off by declaring she could wed no one till she had finished the winding-sheet she was making for old

Laertes, her father-in-law; while to prevent its coming to an end she undid by night whatever she wove by day. Telemachus had gone to seek his father, but came home baffled to Eumæus' hut, and there was allowed to recognise Ulysses. But it was as a beggar, broken-down and foot-sore, that Ulysses sought his palace, and none knew him there but his poor old dog Argus, who licked his feet, and died for joy. The suitors, in their pride, made game of the poor stranger, but Penelope sent for him, in case he brought news of her husband. Even to her he told a feigned story, but she bade the old nurse Euryclea take care of him, and wash his feet. While doing so, the old woman knew him by a scar left by the tusk of a wild boar long ago, and Ulysses could hardly stifle her cry of joy; but she told him all, and who could be trusted among the slaves. The plans were fixed. Telemachus, with much difficulty, persuaded his mother to try to get rid of the suitors by promising to wed him only who could bend Ulysses' bow. One after another tried in vain, and then, amid their sneers, the beggar took it up, and bent it easily, hit the mark, and then aimed it against them! They were all at the banquet-table in the hall. Eumæus and the other faithful servants had closed all the doors, and removed all the arms, and there was a terrible slaughter both of these oppressors and the servants who had joined with them against their queen and her son.

After this, Ulysses made himself known to his wife, and visited his father, who had long retired to his beautiful garden. The kindred of the suitors would have made war on him, but Pallas pacified them, and the Odyssey leaves him to spend his old age in Ithaca, and die a peaceful death. He was just what the Greeks thought a thoroughly brave and wise man; for they had no notion that there was any sin in falsehood and double-dealing.

## CHAP. XI. — THE DOOM OF THE ATRIDES.

You remember that Ulysses met Agamemnon among the other ghosts. The King of Men, as the Iliad calls him, had vast beacons lighted from isle to isle, and from cape to cape, to announce that Troy was won, and that he was on his way home, little knowing what a welcome was in store for him.

His wife Clytemnestra had never forgiven him for the loss of Iphigenia, and had listened to his cousin Ægisthus, who wanted to marry her. She came forth and received Agamemnon with apparent joy, but his poor captive Cassandra wailed aloud, and would not cross the threshold, saying it streamed with blood, and that this was a house of slaughter. No one listened to her, and Agamemnon was led to the bath to refresh himself after his journey. A new embroidered robe lay ready for him, but the sleeves were sewn up at the wrists, and while he could not get his hands free, Ægisthus fell on him and slew him, and poor Cassandra likewise.

His daughter Electra, fearing that her young brother Orestes would not be safe since he was the right heir of the kingdom, sent him secretly away to Phocis, where the king bred him up with his own son Pylades, and the two youths loved each other as much as Achilles and Patroclus had done. It was the bounden duty of a son to be the avenger of his father's blood, and after eight years, as soon as Orestes was a grown warrior, he went with his friend in secret to Mycenæ, and offered a lock of his hair on his father's tomb. Electra, coming out with her offerings, found these tokens, and knew that he was near. He made himself known, and she admitted him into the house, where he fulfilled his stern charge, and killed both Clytemnestra and Ægisthus, then celebrated their funeral rites with all due solemnity.

This was on the very day that Menelaus and Helen returned home. They had been shipwrecked first in Egypt, where they spent eight years, and then were held by contrary winds on a little isle on the coast of Egypt, where they would have been starved if Menelaus had not managed to capture the old sea-god Proteus, when he came up to pasture his flock of seals on the beach, and, holding him tight, while he changed into every kind of queer shape, forced him at last to speak. By Proteus' advice, Menelaus returned to Egypt, and made the sacrifices to the gods he had forgotten before, after which he safely reached Sparta, on the day of Clytemnestra's obsequies. Just as they were ended, the Furies, the avengers of crime, fell upon Orestes for having slain his mother. He fled in misery from Mycenæ, which Menelaus took into his own hands, while the wretched Orestes went from place to place, still attended and comforted by faithful Pylades, but he never tried to rest without being again beset by the Furies. At last Apollo, at the oracle at Delphi, sent him to take his trial at the court of justice at Athens, called Areopagus, Ares' (or Mars') Hill, after which the oracle bade him fetch the image of Diana from Tauris, marry his cousin Hermione, the daughter of Menelaus and Helen, and recover his father's kingdom.

Pallas Athene came down to preside at Areopagus, and directed the judges to pronounce that, though the slaying of a mother was a fearful crime, yet it was Orestes' duty to avenge his father's death. He was therefore acquitted, and purified by sacrifice, and was no more haunted by the Furies, while with Pylades he sailed for Tauris. In that inhospitable place it was the custom to sacrifice all strangers to Diana, and, as soon as they had landed, Orestes and Pylades were seized, and taken to the priestess at the temple, that their hair might be cut and their brows wreathed for the sacrifice. The priestess was no other than Iphigenia, who had been snatched away from Aulis, and, when she and the brother, whom she had left an infant, found each other out, she contrived to leave the temple by night, carrying the image of Diana with her. They went to Delphi together, and there Iphigenia met Electra, who had heard a false report that her beloved Orestes had been sacrificed by the priestess of Tauris, and was just going to tear out her eyes, when Orestes appeared, and the sisters were made known to each other. A temple was built for the image near Marathon, in Attica, and Iphigenia spent the rest of her life as priestess there. Orestes, in the meantime, married Hermione — after, as some say, killing Pyrrhus, the son of Achilles, to whom she was either promised or married — and reigned over both Mycenæ and Sparta until the hundred years' truce with the Heracleids, or grandsons of Hercules, had come to an end, and they returned with a party of Dorians and conquered Sparta, eighty years after the Trojan war.

PLAIN OF SPARTA, WITH MOUNT TAYGETUS.

This is the last of the events of the age of heroes, when so much must be fable, though there may be a germ of historical truth which no one can make out among the old tales that had come from the East, and the like of which may be found among the folk-lore of all nations. These are the most famous of the stories, because they joined all Greeks together, and were believed in by all Greeks alike in their main circumstances; but every state had its own story, and one or two may be told before we end this chapter of myths, because they are often heard of, and poetry has been written about some of them.

At Thebes, in Bœotia, the king, Laius, was told that his first child would be his death. So as soon as it was born he had its ancles pierced, and put it out in a wood to die; but it was found by a shepherd, and brought to Corinth, where the queen named it Œdipus, or Swollen Feet, and bred it up as her own child. Many years later Œdipus set out for the Delphic oracle, to ask who he was; but all the answer he received was that he must shun his native land, for he would be the slayer of his own father. He therefore resolved not to return to Corinth, but on his journey he met in a narrow pass with a chariot going to Delphi. A quarrel arose, and in the fight that followed he slew the man to whom the chariot belonged, little knowing that it was Laius, his own father.

He then went on through Bœotia. On the top of a hill near Thebes sat a monster called the Sphinx, with a women's head, a lion's body, and an eagle's wings. She had been taught riddles by the Muses, and whoever failed to answer them she devoured upon the spot. Whoever could answer her was to marry the king's sister, and share the kingdom. Œdipus went bravely up to her, and heard her question, "What is the animal that is at first four-legged, then two-legged, then three-legged?" "Man," cried Œdipus. "He creeps as a babe on all-fours, walks upright in his prime, and uses a staff in his old age." Thereupon the Sphinx turned to stone, and Œdipus married the princess, and reigned many years, till there was a famine and pestilence, and the oracle was asked the cause. It answered that the land must be purified from the blood of Laius. Only then did Œdipus find out that it was Laius whom he had slain; and then, by the marks on his ancles, it was proved that he was the babe who had been exposed, so that he had fulfilled his fate, and killed his own father. To save Thebes, he left the country, with his eyes put out by way of expiation, and wandered about, only attended by his faithful daughter Antigone, till he came to Athens, where, like Orestes, he was sheltered, and allowed to expiate his crime. After his death, Antigone came back to Thebes, where her two brothers Eteocles and Polynices had agreed to reign each a year by turns; but when Eteocles' year was over he would not give up to his brother, and Polynices, in a rage, collected friends, among whom were six great chiefs, and attacked Thebes. In the battle called "The Seven Chiefs against Thebes," all were slain, and Eteocles and Polynices fell by each other's hands. Their uncle Creon forbade that the bodies of men who had so ruined their country should receive funeral honours from anyone on pain of death, thus condemning their shades to the dreary flitting about on the banks of the Styx, so much dreaded. But their sister Antigone, the noblest woman of Greek imagination, dared the peril, stole forth at night, and gave burial alone to her two brothers. She was found out, and put to death for her sisterly devotion, though Creon's own son killed himself for grief and love of her. This happened in the generation before the Trojan war, for Tydeus, the father of Diomed, was one of the seven chiefs.

Macedon, the country northward of Greece, had one very droll legend. Midas, king of the Bryges, at the foot of Mount Bermion, had a most beautiful garden, full of all kinds of fruit. This was often stolen, until he watched, and found the thief was old Silenus, the tutor of Bacchus. Thereupon he filled with wine the fount where Silenus was used to drink after his feast, and thus, instead of going away, the old god fell asleep, and Midas caught him, and made him answer all his questions. One was, "What is best for man?" and the answer was very sad, "What is best for man is never to have been born. The second best is to die as soon as may be." At last Silenus was released, on condition that he would grant one wish, and this was that all that Midas touched should turn to gold; and so it did, clothes, food, and everything the king took hold of became solid gold, so that he found himself starving, and entreated that the gift might be taken away. So he was told to bathe in the river Pactolus, in Lydia, and the sands became full of gold dust; but, in remembrance of his folly, his ears grew long like those of a donkey. He hid them by wearing a tall Phrygian cap, and no one knew of them but his barber, who was told he should be put to death if ever he mentioned these ears. The barber was so haunted by the secret, that at last he could not help relieving himself, by going to a clump of reeds and whispering into them, "King Midas has the ears of an ass;" and whenever the wind rustled in the reeds, those who went by might always hear them in turn whisper to one another, "King Midas has the ears of an ass." Some accounts say that it was for saying that Pan was a better musician than Apollo that Midas had his ass's ears, and that it was Lydia of which he was king; and this seems most likely, for almost as many Greeks lived in the borders of Asia Minor as lived in Greece itself, and there were many stories of the hills, cities, and rivers there, but I have only told you what is most needful to be known — not, of course, to be believed, but to be known.

## CHAP. XII. — AFTER THE HEROIC AGE.

All these heroes of whom we have been telling lived, if they lived at all, about the time of the Judges of Israel. Troy is thought to have been taken at the time that Saul was reigning in Israel, and there is no doubt that there once was a city between Mount Ida and the Ægean Sea, for quantities of remains have been dug up, and among them many rude earthenware images of an owl, the emblem of Pallas Athene, likenesses perhaps of the Palladium. Hardly anything is told either false or true of Greece for three hundred years after this time, and when something more like history begins we find that all Greece, small as it is, was divided into very small states, each of which had a chief city and a government of its own, and was generally shut in from its neighbours by mountains or by sea. There were the three tribes, Ionian, Dorian, and Æolian, dwelling in these little states, and, though they often quarrelled among themselves, all thinking themselves one nation, together with their kindred in the islands of the Ægean, on the coasts of Asia, and also in Sicily and Southern Italy, which was sometimes called Greater Greece.

Some time between the heroic age and the historical time, there had been a great number of songs and verses composed telling of the gods and heroes. Singers and poets used to be entertained by the kings, and sometimes to wander from one place to another, welcomed by all, as they chanted to the harp or the lyre the story of the great forefathers of their hosts, especially when they had all joined together, as in the hunt of the great boar of Calydon, in the voyage for the Golden Fleece, and, above all, in the siege of Troy. The greatest of all these singers was the blind poet Homer, whose songs of the wrath of Achilles and the wanderings of Ulysses were loved and learnt by everyone. Seven different cities claimed to be his birth-place, but no one knows more about him than that he was blind — not even exactly when he lived — but his poems did much to make the Greeks hold together.

And so did their religion. Everybody sent to ask questions of the oracle of Apollo at Delphi, and there really were answers to them, though no one can tell by what power. And at certain times there were great festivals at certain shrines. One was at Olympia, in Elis, where there was a great festival every five years. It was said that Hercules, when a little boy, had here won a foot-race with his brothers, and when the Heracleids returned to Sparta they founded a feast, with games for all the Greeks to contend in. There were chariot races, horse races, foot races, boxing and wrestling matches, throwing weights, playing with quoits, singing and reciting of poems. The winner was rewarded with a wreath of bay, of pine, of parsley, or the like, and he wore such an one as his badge of honour for the rest of his life. Nothing was thought more of than being first in the Olympic games, and the Greeks even came to make them their measure of time, saying that any event happened in such and such a year of such an Olympiad. The first Olympiad they counted from was the year 776 b.c., that is, before the coming of our blessed Lord. There were other games every three years, which Theseus was said to have instituted, on the isthmus of Corinth, called the Isthmean Games, and others in two different places, and no honour was more highly esteemed than success in these.

There were also councils held of persons chosen from each tribe, called Amphictyons, for arranging their affairs, both religious and worldly, and one great Amphictyonic council, which met near Delphi, to discuss the affairs of all Greece. In truth, all the great nations who long ago parted in Asia have had somewhat the same arrangement. A family grew first into a clan, then into a tribe, then into a nation, and the nation that settled in one country formed fresh family divisions of clans, tribes, and families. At first the father of a family would take council with the sons, the head of a clan with the fathers of families, the chief of a tribe with the heads of clans, and as these heads of clans grew into little kings, the ablest of them would lead the nation in time of war, as Agamemnon did the chiefs against Troy. However, the Greeks seem for the most part, between the heroic and historical ages, to have dropped the king or chief of each state, and only to have managed them by various councils of the chief heads of families, who were called aristoi, the best, while those who were not usually called into council, though they too were free, and could choose their governors, and vote in great matters, were termed demos, the people. This is why we hear of aristocracy and democracy. Under these freemen were the people of the country they had conquered, or any slaves they had bought or taken captive, or strangers who had come to live in the place, and these had no rights at all.

Greek cities were generally beautiful places, in valleys between the hills and the sea. They were sure to have several temples to the gods of the place. These were colonnades of stone-pillars, upon steps, open all round, but with a small dark cell in the middle, which was the shrine of the god, whose statue, and carvings of whose adventures, adorned the outside. There was an altar in the open-air for sacrifices, the flesh of which was afterwards eaten. In the middle of a town was always a market-place, which served as the assembling-place of the people, and it had a building attached to it where the fire of Vesta was never allowed to go out. The charge of it was given to the best men who could be found; and when a set of citizens went forth to make a new home or colony in Asia, Sicily, or Italy, they always took brands from this fire, guarded them carefully in a censer, and lighted their altar-fires therefrom when they settled down.

GREEK INTERIOR.

These cities were of houses built round paved courts. The courts had generally a fountain in the middle, and an altar to the hero forefather of the master, where, before each meal, offerings were made and wine poured out. The rooms were very small, and used for little but sleeping; and the men lived chiefly in the cloister or pillared walks round the court. There was a kind of back-court for the women of the family, who did not often appear in the front one, though they were not shut up like Eastern women. Most Greeks had farms, which they worked by the help of their slaves, and whence came the meat, corn, wine, and milk that maintained the family. The women spun the wool of the sheep, wove and embroidered it, making for the men short tunics reaching to the knee, with a longer mantle for dignity or for need; and for themselves long robes reaching to the feet — a modest and graceful covering — but leaving the arms bare. Men cut their hair close; women folded their tresses round their heads in the simplest and most becoming manner that has yet been invented. The feet were bare, but sandalled, and the sandals fastened with ornamented thongs. Against the sun sometimes a sort of hat was worn, or the mantle was put over the head, and women had thick veils wrapping them.

GREEK ROBE.

In time of war the armour was a helmet with a horse-hair crest, a breast-plate on a leathern cuirass, which had strips of leather hanging from the lower edge as far down as the knee; sometimes greaves to guard the leathern buskin; a round shield of leather, faced with metal, and often beautifully ornamented; and also spears, swords, daggers, and sometimes bows and arrows. Chariots for war had been left off since the heroic times; indeed Greece was so hilly that horses were not very much used in battle, though riding was part of the training of a Greek, and the Thessalian horses were much valued. Every state that had a seaboard had its fleet of galleys, with benches of oars; but the Greek sailors seldom ventured out of sight of land, and all that Greece or Asia Minor did not produce was brought by the Phœnicians, the great sailors, merchants, and slave-dealers of the Old World. They brought Tyrian purple, gold of Ophir, silver of Spain, tin of Gaul and Britain, ivory from India, and other such luxuries; and they also bought captives in war, or kidnapped children on the coast, and sold them as slaves. Ulysses' faithful swineherd was such a slave, and of royal birth; and such was the lot of many an Israelite child, for whom its parents' "eyes failed with looking and longing."

MALE COSTUME.

The Greeks had more power of thought and sense of grace than any other people have ever had. They always had among them men seeking for truth and beauty. The truth-seekers were called philosophers, or lovers of wisdom. They were always trying to understand about God and man, and this world, and guessing at something great, far beyond the stories of Jupiter; and they used to gather young men round them under the pillared porches and talk over these thoughts, or write them in beautiful words. Almost all the sciences began with the Greeks; their poems and their histories are wonderfully written; and they had such great men among them that, though most of their little states were smaller than an ordinary English county, and the whole of them together do not make a country as large as Ireland, their history is the most remarkable in the world, except that of the Jews. The history of the Jews shows what God does for men; the history of Greece shows what man does left to himself.

Greece was not so small as what is called Greece now in our modern maps. It reached northwards as far as the Volutza and Khimera mountains, beyond which lay Macedon, where the people called themselves Greeks, but were not quite accepted as such. In this peninsula, together with the Peloponnesus and the isles, there were twenty little states, making up Hellas, or Greece. [2]

## CHAP. XIII. — LYCURGUS AND THE LAWS OF SPARTA.
### b.c. 884–668.

You remember that after a hundred years the grandsons of Hercules returned, bringing with them their followers of Dorian birth, and conquered Laconia. These Dorians called themselves Spartans, and were the rulers of the land, though the Greeks, who were there before them, were also freemen, all but those of one city, called Helos, which revolted, and was therefore broken up, and the people were called Helots, and became slaves to the Spartans. One of the Spartan kings, sons of Hercules, had twin sons, and these two reigned together with equal rights, and so did their sons after them, so that there were always two kings at Sparta. One line was called the Agids, from Agis, its second king; the other Eurypontids, from Eurypon, its third king, instead of from the two original twins.

The affairs of Sparta had fallen into a corrupt state by the third generation after Eurypon. The king of his line was killed in a quarrel, and his widow, a wicked woman, offered his brother Lycurgus to kill her little new-born babe, if he would marry her, that she might continue to be queen. Lycurgus did not show his horror, but advised her to send the child alive to him, that he might dispose of it. So far from killing it was he, that he carried it at once to the council, placed it on the throne, and proclaimed it as Charilaus, king of Sparta.

There were still murmurs from those who did not know that Lycurgus had saved the little boy's life. As he was next heir to the throne, it was thought that he must want to put Charilaus out of the way, so as to reign himself; so, having seen the boy in safe keeping, Lycurgus went on his travels to study the laws and ways of other countries. He visited Crete, and learnt the laws of Minos; and, somewhere among the Greek settlements in Asia, he is said to have seen and talked to Homer, and heard his songs. He also went to Egypt, and after that to India, where he may have learnt much from the old Brahmin philosophy; and then, having made his plan, he repaired to Delphi, and prayed until he received answer from Apollo that his laws should be the best, and the state that obeyed them the most famous in Greece. He then went home, where he had been much missed, for his young nephew Charilaus, though grown to man's estate, was too weak and good-natured to be much obeyed, and there was a great deal of idleness, and gluttony, and evil of all sorts prevailing.

Thirty Spartans bound themselves to help Lycurgus in his reform, and Charilaus, fancying it a league against himself, fled into the temple of Pallas, but his uncle fetched him out, and told him that he only wanted to make laws for making the Spartans great and noble. The rule was only for the real Dorian Spartans, the masters of the country, and was to make them perfect warriors. First, then, he caused all the landmarks to be taken up, and the lands thrown into one, which he divided again into lots, each of which was large enough to yield 82 bushels of corn in a year, with wine and oil in proportion. Then, to hinder hoarding, he allowed no money to be used in the country but great iron weights, so that a small sum took up a great deal of room, and could hardly be carried about, and thus there was no purchasing Phœnician luxuries; nor was anyone to use gold or ivory, soft cushions, carpets, or the like, as being unworthy of the race of Hercules. The whole Spartan nation became, in fact, a regiment of highly-disciplined warriors. They were to live together in public barracks, only now and then visiting their homes, and even when they slept there, being forbidden to touch food till they came to the general meal, which was provided for by contributions of meal, cheese, figs, and wine from each man's farm, and a little money to buy fish and meat; also a sort of soup called black broth, which was so unsavoury that nobody but a Spartan could eat it, because it was said they brought the best sauce, namely, hunger. A boy was admitted as soon as he was old enough, and was warned against repeating the talk of his elders, by being told on his first entrance, by the eldest man in the company, "Look you, sir; nothing said here goes out there." Indeed no one used more words than needful, so that short, pithy sayings came to be called Laconic. To be a perfect soldier was the great point, so boys were taught that no merit was greater than bearing pain without complaint; and they carried this so far, that a boy who had brought a young wolf into the hall, hidden under his tunic, let it bite him even to death without a groan or cry. It is said that they were trained to theft, and were punished, not for the stealing, but the being found out. And, above all, no Spartan was ever to turn his back in battle. The mothers gave the sons a shield, with the words, "With it, or on it." The Spartan shields were long, so that a dead warrior would be borne home on his shield; but a man would not dare show his face again if he had thrown it away in flight. The women were trained to running, leaping, and throwing the bar, like the men, and were taught stern hardihood, so that, when their boys were offered to the cruel Diana, they saw them flogged to death at her altar without a tear. All the lives of the Spartans were spent in exercising for war, and the affairs of the state were managed not so much by the kings, but by five judges called Ephors, who were chosen every year, while the kings had very little power. They had to undergo the same discipline as the rest — dressed, ate, and lived like them; but they were the high priests and chief captains, and made peace or war.

At first Lycurgus' laws displeased some of the citizens much, and, when he was proposing them, a young man named Alcander struck him on the face with his staff, and put out his eye. The others were shocked, and put Alcander into Lycurgus' hands, to be punished as he thought fit. All Lycurgus did was to make him wait upon him at meals, and Alcander was so touched and won over that he became one of his best supporters. After having fully taught Sparta to observe his rule, Lycurgus declared that he had another journey to take, and made the people swear to observe his laws till he came back again. He never did come back, and they held themselves bound by them for ever.

This story of Lycurgus has been doubted, but whether there were such a man or not, it is quite certain that these were the laws of Sparta in her most famous days, and that they did their work of making brave and hardy soldiers. The rule was much less strict in the camp than the city, and the news of a war was delightful to the Spartans as a holiday-time. All the hard work of their farms was done for them by the Helots, who were such a strong race that it was not easy to keep them down, although their masters were very cruel to them, often killing large numbers of them if they seemed to be growing dangerous, always ill-treating them, and, it is said, sometimes making them drunk, that the sight of their intoxication might disgust the young

Spartans. In truth, the whole Spartan system was hard and unfeeling, and much fitter to make fighting machines than men.

The first great Spartan war that we know of was with their neighbours of Messenia, who stood out bravely, but were beaten, and brought down to the state of Helots in the year 723 b.c., all but a small band, who fled into other states. Among them was born a brave youth named Aristomenes, who collected all the boldest of his fellow-Messenians to try to save their country, and Argos, Arcadia, and Elis joined with them. Several battles were fought. One, which was called the battle of the Boar's Pillar, was long sung about. An augur had told Aristomenes that under a tree sat the Spartan brothers Castor and Pollux, to protect their countrymen, and that he might not pass it; but in the pursuit he rushed by it, and at that moment the shield was rent from him by an unseen hand. While he was searching for it, the Spartans (who do seem this time to have fled) escaped; but Messene was free, and he was crowned with flowers by the rejoicing women. A command from Apollo made him descend into a cave, where he found his shield, adorned with the figure of an eagle, and, much encouraged, he won another battle, and would have entered Sparta itself, had not Helen and her twin brothers appeared to warn him back. At last, however, the war turned against him, and in a battle on Laconian ground he was stunned by a stone, and taken prisoner, with 50 more. They were all condemned to be thrown down a high rock into a deep pit. Everyone else was killed by the fall, but Aristomenes found himself unhurt, with sky above, high precipices on all sides, and his dead comrades under him. He wrapped himself in his cloak to wait for death, but on the third day he heard something moving, uncovered his face, and saw that a fox had crept in from a cavern at the side of the pit. He took hold of the fox's tail, crawled after it, and at last saw the light of day. He scraped the earth till the way was large enough for him to pass, escaped, and gathered his friends, to the amazement of the Spartans. Again he gained the victory, and a truce was made, but he was treacherously seized, and thrown into prison. However, this time he was set free by a maiden, whom he gave in marriage to his son. At last Eira, the chief city of Messenia, was betrayed by a foolish woman, while Aristomenes was laid aside by a wound. In spite of this, however, he fought for three days and nights against the Spartans, and at last drew up all the survivors — women as well as men — in a hollow square, with the children in the middle, and demanded a free passage. The Spartans allowed these brave

Messenians to pass untouched, and they reached Arcadia. There the dauntless Aristomenes arranged another scheme for seizing Sparta itself, but it was betrayed, and failed. The Arcadians stoned the traitor, while the gentle Aristomenes wept for him. The remaining Messenians begged him to lead them to a new country, but he would not leave Greece as long as he could strike a blow against Sparta. However, he sent his two sons, and they founded in Sicily a new Messene, which we still call Messina. Aristomenes waited in vain in Arcadia, till Damagetus, king of Rhodes, who had been bidden by an oracle to marry the daughter of the best of Greeks, asked for the daughter of Aristomenes, and persuaded him to finish his life in peace and honour in Rhodes.

## CHAP. XIV. — SOLON AND THE LAWS OF ATHENS.
### b.c. 594–546.

North of the Peloponnesus, jutting out into the Ægean Sea, lay the rocky little Ionian state of Attica, with its lovely city, Athens. There was a story that Neptune and Pallas Athene had had a strife as to which should be the patron of the city, and that it was to be given to whichever should produce the most precious gift for it. Neptune struck the earth with his trident, and there appeared a war-horse; but Pallas' touch brought forth an olive-tree, and this was judged the most useful gift. The city bore her name; the tiny Athenian owl was her badge; the very olive-tree she had bestowed was said to be that which grew in the court of the Acropolis, a sacred citadel on a rock above the city; and near at hand was her temple, called the Parthenon, or Virgin's Shrine. Not far off was the Areopagus, a Hill of Ares, or Mars, the great place for hearing causes and doing justice; and below these there grew up a city filled with men as brave as the Spartans, and far more thoughtful and wise, besides having a most perfect taste and sense of beauty.

GATE OF MYCENAE.

The Athenians claimed Theseus as their greatest king and first lawgiver. It was said that, when the Dorians were conquering the Peloponnesus, they came north and attacked Attica, but were told by an oracle that they never would succeed if they slew the king of Athens. Codrus, who was then king of Athens, heard of this oracle, and devoted himself for his country. He found that in battle the Dorians always forbore to strike him, and he therefore disguised himself, went into the enemy's camp, quarrelled with a soldier there, and thus caused himself to be killed, so as to save his country. He was the last king. The Athenians would not have anyone less noble to sit in his seat, and appointed magistrates called Archons in the stead of kings.

Soon they fell into a state of misrule and disorder, and they called on a philosopher named Draco to draw up laws for them. Draco's laws were good, but very strict, and for the least crime the punishment was death. Nobody could keep them, so they were set aside and forgotten, and confusion grew worse, till another wise lawgiver named Solon undertook to draw up a fresh code of laws for them.

Solon was one of the seven wise men of Greece, who all lived at the same time. The other six were Thales, Bion, Pittacus, Cleobulus, Chilo, and Periander. This last was called Tyrant of Corinth. When the ancient Greeks spoke of a tyrant, they did not mean a cruel king so much as a king who had not been heir to the crown, but had taken to himself the rule over a free people. A very curious story belongs to Periander, for we have not quite parted with the land of fable. It is about the poet Arion, who lived chiefly with him at Corinth, but made one voyage to Sicily. As he was coming back, the sailors plotted to throw him overboard, and divide the gifts he was bringing with him. When he found they were resolved, he only begged to play once more on his lyre; then, standing on the prow, he played and sung a hymn calling the gods to his aid. So sweet were the sounds that shoals of dolphins came round the ship, and Arion, leaping from the prow, placed himself on the back of one, which bore him safely to land. Periander severely punished the treacherous sailors. Some think that this story was a Greek alteration of the history of Jonah, which might have been brought by the Phœnician sailors.

Solon was Athenian by birth, and of the old royal line. He had served his country in war, and had travelled to study the habits of other lands, when the Athenians, wearied with the oppressions of the rich and great, and finding that no one attended to the laws of Draco, left it to him to form a new constitution. It would be of no use to try to explain it all. The chief thing to be remembered about it is, that at the head of the government were nine chief magistrates, who were called Archons, and who were changed every three years. To work with them, there was a council of four hundred aristoi, or nobles; but when war or peace was decided, the whole demos, or people, had to vote, according to their tribes; and if a man was thought to be dangerous to the state, the demos might sentence him to be banished. His name was written on an oyster shell, or on a tile, by those who wished him to be driven away, and these were thrown into one great vessel. If they amounted to a certain number, the man was said to be "ostracised," and forced to leave the city. This was sometimes done very unjustly, but it answered the purpose of sending away rich men who became overbearing, and kept tyrants from rising up. There were no unnatural laws as there were at Sparta; people might live at home as they pleased; but there were schools, and all the youths were to be taught there, both learning and training in all exercises. And whether it was from Solon's laws or their own character, there certainly did arise in Athens some of the greatest and noblest men of all times.

After having set things in order, Solon is said to have been so annoyed by foolish questions on his schemes, that he went again on his travels. First he visited his friend Thales, at Miletus, in Asia Minor; and, finding him rich and comfortable, he asked why he had never married. Thales made no answer then, but a few days later he brought in a stranger, who, he said, was just from Athens. Solon asked what was the news. "A great funeral was going on, and much lamentation," said the man. "Whose was it?" He did not learn the name, but it was a young man of great promise, whose father was abroad upon his travels. "The father was much famed for his wisdom and justice." "Was it Solon?" cried the listener. "It was." Solon burst into tears, tore his hair, and beat his breast; but Thales took his hand, saying, "Now you see, O Solon, why I have never married, lest I should expose myself to griefs such as these;" and then told him it was all a trick. Solon could not much have approved such a trick, for when Thespis, a great actor of plays, came to Athens, Solon asked him if he were not ashamed to speak so many falsehoods. Thespis answered that it was all in sport. "Ay," said Solon, striking his staff on the ground; "but he that tells lies in sport will soon tell them in earnest."

After this, Solon went on to Lydia. This was a kingdom of Greek settlers in Asia Minor, where flowed that river Pactolus, whose sands contained gold-dust, from King Midas' washing, as the story went. The king was Crœsus, who was exceedingly rich and splendid. He welcomed Solon, and, after showing him all his glory, asked whom the philosopher thought the happiest of men. "An honest man named Tellus," said Solon, "who lived uprightly, was neither rich nor poor, had good children, and died bravely for his country." Crœsus was vexed, but asked who was next happiest. "Two brothers named Cleobis and Bito," said Solon, "who were so loving and dutiful to their mother, that, when she wanted to go to the temple of Juno, they yoked themselves to her car, and drew her thither; then, having given this proof of their love, they lay down to sleep, and so died without pain or grief." "And what do you think of me?" said Crœsus. "Ah!" said Solon, "call no man happy till he is dead."

Crœsus was mortified at such a rebuff to his pride, and neglected Solon. There was a clever crooked Egyptian slave at Crœsus' court, called Æsop, who gave his advice in the form of the fables we know so well, such as the wolf and the lamb, the fox and the grapes, etc.; though, as the Hindoos and Persians have from old times told the same stories, it would seem as if Æsop only repeated them, but did not invent them. When Æsop saw Solon in the background, he said, "Solon, visits to kings should be seldom, or else pleasant." "No," said Solon; "visits to kings should be seldom, or else profitable," as the courtly slave found them. Æsop came to a sad end. Crœsus sent him to Delphi to distribute a sum of money among the poor, but they quarrelled so about it that Æsop said he should take it back to the king, and give none at all; whereupon the Delphians, in a rage, threw him off a precipice, and killed him.

Crœsus was just thinking of going to war with the great Cyrus, king of the Medes and Persians, the same who overcame Assyria, took Babylon, and restored Jerusalem, and who was now subduing Asia Minor. Crœsus asked council of all the oracles, but first he tried their truth. He bade his messenger ask the oracle at Delphi what he was doing while they were inquiring. The answer was —

"Lo, on my sense striketh the smell of a shell-covered tortoise Boiling on the fire, with the flesh of a lamb, in a cauldron; Brass is the vessel below, brass the cover above it."

Crœsus was really, as the most unlikely thing to be guessed, boiling a tortoise and a lamb together in a brazen vessel. Sure now of the truth of the oracle, he sent splendid gifts, and asked whether he should go to war with Cyrus. The answer was that, if he did, a mighty kingdom would be overthrown.

He thought it meant the Persian, but it was his own. Lydia was overcome, Sardis, his capital, was burnt, and he was about to be slain, when, remembering the warning, "Call no man happy till his death," he cried out, "O Solon, Solon, Solon!"

Cyrus heard him, and bade that he should be asked what it meant. The story so struck the great king, that he spared Crœsus, and kept him as his adviser for the rest of his life.

## CHAP. XV. — PISISTRATUS AND HIS SONS. b.c. 558–499.

After all the pains that Solon had taken to guard the freedom of the Athenians, his system had hardly begun to work before his kinsman Pisistratus, who was also of the line of Codrus, overthrew it. First this man pretended to have been nearly murdered, and obtained leave to have a guard of fifty men, armed with clubs; and with these he made everyone afraid of him, so that he had all the power, and became tyrant of Athens. He was once driven out, but he found a fine, tall, handsome woman, a flower-girl, in one of the villages of Attica, dressed her in helmet and cuirass, like the goddess Pallas, and came into Athens in a chariot with her, when she presented him to the people as their ruler. The common people thought she was their goddess, and Pisistratus had friends among the rich, so he recovered his power, and he did not, on the whole, use it badly. He made a kind law, decreeing that a citizen who had been maimed in battle should be provided for by the State, and he was the first Greek to found a library, and collect books — namely, manuscripts upon the sheets of the rind of the Egyptian paper-rush, or else upon skins. He was also the first person to collect and arrange the poems of Homer. Everybody seems to have known some part by heart, but they were in separate songs, and Pisistratus first had them written down and put in order, after which no Greek was thought an educated man unless he thoroughly knew the Iliad and Odyssey.

Pisistratus ruled for thirty-three years, and made the Athenians content, and when he died his sons Hippias and Hipparchus ruled much as he had done, and gave no cause for complaint. One thing they did was to set up mile-stones all over the roads of Attica, each with a bust of Mercury on the top, and a wise proverb carved below the number of the miles. But they grew proud and insolent, and one day a damsel of high family was rudely sent away from a solemn religious procession, because Hipparchus had a quarrel with her brother Harmodius. This only made Harmodius vow vengeance, and, together with his friend Aristogeiton, he made a plot with other youths for surrounding the two brothers at a great festival, when everyone carried myrtle-boughs, as well as their swords and shields. The conspirators had daggers hidden in the myrtle, and succeeded in killing Hipparchus, but Harmodius was killed on the spot, and Aristogeiton was taken and tortured to make him reveal his other accomplices, and so was a girl named Lecena, who was known to have been in their secrets; but she bore all the pain without a word, and when it was over she was found to have bitten off her tongue, that she might not betray her friends. Hippias kept up his rule for a few years longer, but he found all going against him, and that the people were bent on having Solon's system back; so, fearing for his life, he sent away his wife and children, and soon followed them to Asia, b.c. 510. This — which is called the Expulsion of the Pisistratids — was viewed by the Athenians as the beginning of their freedom. They paid yearly honours to the memory of the murderers Harmodius and Aristogeiton; and as Lecena means a lioness, they honoured that brave woman's constancy with the statue of a lioness without a tongue.

Hippias wandered about for some time, and ended by going to the court of the king of Persia. Cyrus was now dead, after having established a great empire, which spread from the Persian Gulf to the shore of the Mediterranean, and had Babylon for one of its capitals. When Crœsus was conquered, almost all the Greek colonies along the coast of Asia Minor likewise fell to the "Great King," as his subjects called him. The Persians adored the sun and fire as emblems of the great God, and thought the king himself had something of divinity in his person, and therefore, like most Eastern kings, he had entire power over his people for life or death; they were all his slaves, and the only thing he could not do was to change his own decrees.

SHORES OF THE PERSIAN GULF.

After the Asian coast, the isles of the Ægean stood next in the way of the Persian. In the little isle of Samos lived a king called Polycrates, who had always been wealthy and prosperous. His friend Amasis, king of Egypt, told him that the gods were always jealous of the fortunate, and that, if he wished to avert some terrible disaster, he had better give up something very precious. Upon this Polycrates took off his beautiful signet ring and threw it into the sea; but a few days later a large fish was brought as a present to the king, and when it was cut up the ring was found in its stomach, and restored to Polycrates. Upon this Amasis renounced his friendship, declaring that, as the gods threw back his offering, something dreadful was before him. The foreboding came sadly true, for the Persian satrap, or governor, of Sardis, being envious of Polycrates, declared that the Ionian was under the Great King's displeasure, and invited him to Sardis to clear himself. Polycrates set off, but was seized as soon as he landed in Asia, and hung upon a cross.

Amasis himself died just as the Persians were coming to attack Egypt, which Cyrus' son Cambyses entirely conquered, and added to the Persian empire; but Cambyses shortly after lost his senses and died, and there was an unsettled time before a very able and spirited king named Darius obtained the crown, and married Cyrus' daughter Atossa. Among the prisoners made at Samos there was a physician named Democedes, who was taken to Susa, Darius' capital. He longed to get home, and tried not to show how good a doctor he was; but the king one day hurt his foot, and, when all the Persian doctors failed to cure him, he sent for Democedes, who still pretended to be no wiser, until torture was threatened, and he was forced to try his skill. Darius recovered, made him great gifts, and sent him to attend his wives; but Democedes still pined for home, and managed to persuade Atossa to beg the king to give her Spartan and Athenian slaves, and to tell him some great undertaking was expected from him. The doctor's hope in this was that he should be sent as a spy to Greece, before the war, and should make his escape; but it was a bad way of showing love to his country. Hippias was at Susa too, trying to stir up Darius to attack Athens, and restore him as a tributary king; and there was also Histiæus, a Greek, who had been tyrant of Miletus, and who longed to get home. All the Ionian Greeks on the coast of Asia Minor hated the Persian rule, and Histiæus hoped that if they revolted he should be wanted there, so he sent a letter to his friend Aristagoras, at Miletus, in a most curious way. He had the head of a trusty slave shaved, then, with a red-hot pin, wrote his advice to rise against the Persians, and, when the hair was grown again, sent the man as a present to Aristagoras, with orders to tell him to shave his head.

Aristagoras read the letter, and went to Sparta to try to get the help of the kings in attacking Persia. He took with him a brass plate, engraven with a map of the world, according to the notions of the time, where it looked quite easy to march to Susa, and win the great Eastern empire. At first Cleomenes, the most spirited of the kings, was inclined to listen, but when he found that this easy march would take three months he changed his mind, and thought it beyond Spartan powers. Aristagoras went secretly to his house, and tried to bribe him, at least, to help the Ionians in their rising; but while higher and higher offers were being made, Gorgo, the little daughter of Cleomenes, only eight years old, saw by their looks that something was wrong, and cried out, "Go away, father; this stranger will do you harm." Cleomenes took it as the voice of an oracle, and left the stranger to himself.

He then went to Athens, and the Athenians, being Ionians themselves, listened more willingly, and promised to aid their brethren in freeing themselves. Together, the Athenians and a large body of

Ephesians, Milesians, and other Ionians, attacked Sardis. The Persian satrap Artaphernes threw himself into the citadel; but the town, which was built chiefly of wicker-work, that the houses might not be easily thrown down by earthquakes, caught fire, and was totally burnt. The Athenians could not stay in the flaming streets, and had to give back, and the whole Persian force of the province came up and drove them out. Darius was furious when he heard of the burning of Sardis, and, for fear he should forget his revenge, ordered that a slave should mention the name of Athens every day to him as he sat down to dinner. Histiæus, however, succeeded in his plan, for Darius believed him when he said the uproar could only have broken out in his absence, and let him go home to try to put it down.

He was not very well received by Artaphernes, who was sure he was at the bottom of the revolt. "Aristagoras put on the shoe," he said, "but it was of your stitching."

Aristagoras had been killed, and Histiæus, fleeing to the Ionians, remained with them till they were entirely beaten, and he surrendered to the Persians, by whom he was crucified, while the Ionians were entirely crushed, and saw their fairest children carried off to be slaves in the palace at Susa. Darius had longed after Greek slaves ever since he had seen a fine handsome girl walking along, upright, with a pitcher of water on her head, the bridle of a horse she was leading over her arm, and her hands busy with a distaff. He did not know that such grand people are never found in enslaved, oppressed countries, like his own, and he wanted to have them all under his power, so he began to raise his forces from all parts of his empire, for the conquest of what seemed to him the insolent little cities of Greece, and Hippias, now an old man, undertook to show him the way to Athens, and to betray his country. The battle was between the East and West — between a despot ruling mere slaves, and free, thoughtful cities, full of evil indeed, and making many mistakes, but brave and resolute, and really feeling for their hearths and homes.

## CHAP. XVI. — THE BATTLE OF MARATHON. b.c. 490.

The whole Persian fleet, manned by Phœnician sailors, and a huge army, under the two satraps Datis and Artaphernes, were on the opposite side of the Ægean Sea, ready to overwhelm little Attica first, and then all Greece. Nobody had yet stood firm against those all-conquering Persians, and as they came from island to island the inhabitants fled or submitted. Attica was so small as to have only 9000 fighting men to meet this host. They sent to ask the aid of the Spartans, but though these would have fought bravely, an old rule forbade them to march during the week before the full moon, and in this week Athens might be utterly ruined. Nobody did come to their help but 600 men from the very small state of Platæa, and this little army, not numbering 10,000, were encamped around the temple of Hercules, looking down upon the bay of Marathon, where lay the ships which had just landed at least 200,000 men of all the Eastern nations, and among them many of the Greeks of Asia Minor. The hills slant back so as to make a sort of horse-shoe round the bay, with about five miles of clear flat ground between them and the sea, and on this open space lay the Persians.

It was the rule among the Athenians that the heads of their ten tribes should command by turns each for a day, but Aristides, the best and most high-minded of all of them, persuaded the rest to give up their turns to Miltiades, who was known to be the most skilful captain. He drew up his men in a line as broad as the whole front of the Persian army, though far less deep, and made them all come rushing down at them with even step, but at a run, shouting the war-cry, "Io pæan! Io pæan!" In the middle, where the best men of the Persians were, they stood too firm to be thus broken, but at the sides they gave way, and ran back towards the sea, or over the hills, and then Miltiades gave a signal to the two side divisions — wings, as they were called — to close up together, and crush the Persian centre. The enemy now thought of nothing but reaching their ships and putting out to sea, while the Athenians tried to seize their ships; Cynegyrus, one brave Greek, caught hold of the prow of one ship, and when the crew cut off his hand with an axe, he still clung with the other, till that too was cut off, and he sank and was drowned. The fleet still held many men, and the Athenians saw that, instead of crossing back to Asia Minor, it was sailing round the promontory of Sunium, as if to attack Athens. It was even said that a friend of Hippias had raised a shield, glittering in the sun, as a signal that all the men were away. However, Miltiades left Aristides, with his tribe of 1000 men, to guard the plain and bury the dead, and marched back over the hills with the rest to guard their homes, that same night; but the Persians must have been warned, or have changed their mind, for they sailed away for Asia; and Hippias, who seems to have been wounded in the battle, died at Lemnos. The Spartans came up just as all was over, and greatly praised the Athenians, for indeed it was the first time Greeks had beaten Persians, and it was the battle above all others that saved Europe from falling under the slavery of the East. The fleet was caught by a storm as it crossed the Ægean Sea again.

All the Athenians who had been slain were buried under one great mound, adorned with ten pillars bearing their names; the Platæans had another honourable mound, and the Persians a third. All the treasure that was taken in the camp and ships was honourably brought to the city and divided. There was only one exception, namely, one Kallias, who wore long hair bound with a fillet, and was taken for a king by a poor Persian, who fell on his knees before him, and showed him a well where was a great deal of gold hidden. Kallias not only took the gold, but killed the poor stranger, and his family were ever after held as disgraced, and called by a nickname meaning, "Enriched by the Well."

The Platæans were rewarded by being made freemen of Athens, as well as of their own city; and Miltiades, while all his countrymen were full of joy and exultation, asked of them a fleet of seventy ships, promising to bring them fame and riches. With it he sailed for the island of Faros, that which was specially famed for its white marble. He said he meant to punish the Parians for having joined the Persians, but it really was because of a quarrel of his own. He landed, and required the Parians to pay him a hundred talents, and when they refused he besieged the city, until a woman named Timo, who was priestess at a temple of Ceres near the gates, promised to tell him a way of taking the city if he would meet her at night in the temple, where no man was allowed to enter. He came, and leaped over the outer fence of the temple, but, brave as he was in battle, terror at treading on forbidden and sacred ground overpowered him, and, without seeing the priestess, he leaped back again, fell on the other side, and severely injured his thigh. The siege was given up, and he was carried back helpless to Athens, where there was no mercy to failures, and he was arraigned before the Areopagus assembly, by a man named Xanthippus, for having wasted the money of the State and deceived the people, and therefore being guilty of death.

It must have been a sad thing to see the great captain, who had saved his country in that great battle only a year or two before, lying on his couch, too ill to defend himself, while his brother spoke for him, and appealed to his former services. In consideration of these it was decided not to condemn him to die, but he was, instead, to pay fifty talents of silver, and before the sum could be raised, he died of his hurts. It was said that his son Kimôn put himself into prison till the fine could be raised, so as to release his father's corpse, which was buried with all honour on the plain of Marathon, with a tomb recording his glory, and not his fall.

The two chief citizens who were left were Aristides and Themistocles, both very able men; but Aristides was perfectly high-minded, unselfish, and upright, while Themistocles cared for his own greatness more than anything else. Themistocles was so clever that his tutor had said to him when he was a child, "Boy, thou wilt never be an ordinary person; thou wilt either be a mighty blessing or a mighty curse to thy country." When he grew up he used his powers of leading the multitude for his own advantage, and that of his party. "The gods forbid," he said, "that I should sit on any tribunal where my friends should not have more advantage than strangers." While, on the other hand, Aristides was so impartial and single-hearted that he got the name of Aristides the Just. He cared most for the higher class, the aristoi, and thought they could govern best, while Themistocles sought after the favour of the people; and they both led the minds of the Athenians so completely while they were speaking, that, after a meeting where they had both made a speech, Aristides said, "Athens will never be safe till Themistocles and I are both in prison," meaning that either of them could easily make himself tyrant.

However, Aristides, though of high family, was very poor, and men said it was by the fault of his cousin Kallias, the "Enriched by the Well;" and Themistocles contrived to turn people's minds against him, so as to have him ostracised. One day he met a man in the street, with a shell in his hand, who asked him to write the name of Aristides on it, as he could not write himself. "Pray," said Aristides, "what harm has this person done you, that you wish to banish him?"

"No harm at all," said the man; "only I am sick of always hearing him called the Just."

Aristides had no more to say, but wrote his own name; and six thousand shells having been counted up against him, he was obliged to go into exile for ten years.

Cynegyrus, the man whose hands had been cut off in the bay of Marathon, had a very famous brother named Æschylus — quite as brave a soldier, and a poet besides. The Athenians had come to worshipping Bacchus, but not in the horrid, mad, drunken manner of the first orgies. They had songs and dances by persons with their heads wreathed in vine and ivy leaves, and a goat was sacrificed in the midst. The Greek word for a goat is tragos, and the dances came to be called tragedies. Then came in the custom of having poetical speeches in the midst of the dances, made in the person of some old hero or god, and these always took place in a curve in the side of a hill, so worked out by art that the rock was cut into galleries, for half-circles of spectators to sit one above the other, while the dancers and speakers were on the flat space at the bottom. Thespis, whom Solon reproved for falsehoods, was the first person who made the dancers and singers, who were called the chorus, so answer one another and the speakers that the tragedy became a play, representing some great action of old. The actors had to wear brazen masks and tall buskins, or no one could have well seen or heard them. Æschylus, when a little boy, was set to watch the grapes in his father's vineyard. He fell asleep, and dreamt that Bacchus appeared to him, and bade him make his festivals noble with tragedies; and this he certainly did, for the poetry he wrote for them is some of the grandest that man ever sung, and shows us how these great Greeks were longing and feeling after the truth, like blind men groping in the dark. The custom was to have three grave plays or tragedies on the same subject on three successive days, and then to finish with a droll one, or comedy, as it was called, in honour of the god Comus. There is one trilogy of Æschylus still preserved to us, where we have the death of Agamemnon, the vengeance of Orestes, and his expiation when pursued by the Furies, but the comedy belonging to them is lost.

Almost all the greatest and best Greeks of this time believed in part in the philosophy of Pythagoras, who had lived in the former century, and taught that the whole universe was one great divine musical instrument, as it were, in which stars, sun, winds, and earth did their part, and that man ought to join himself into the same sweet harmony. He thought that if a man did ill his spirit went into some animal, and had a fresh trial to purify it, but it does not seem as if many others believed this notion.

VIEW IN THE VICINITY OF ATHENS.

## CHAP. XVII. — THE EXPEDITION OF XERXES. b.c. 480.

The Athenians had not a long breathing-time. Darius, indeed, died five years after the battle of Marathon; but his son Xerxes was far more fiery and ambitious, and was no sooner on the throne than he began to call together all the vast powers of the East, not to crush Athens alone, but all the Greeks. He was five years gathering them together, but in the spring of 480 he set out from Sardis to march to the Hellespont, where he had a bridge of ships chained together, made to enable his army to cross the strait on foot. Xerxes was a hot-tempered man, not used to resistance, and it was said that when a storm broke part of his bridge he caused the waves to be scourged and fetters to be thrown in, to show that he was going to bind it to his will. He sat on a throne to watch his armies pass by. It is said that there were two million six hundred thousand men, of every speech and dress in Asia and Egypt, with all sorts of weapons; and as the "Great King" watched the endless number pass by, he burst into tears to think how soon all this mighty host would be dead men!

Xerxes had a huge fleet besides, manned by Phœnicians and Greeks of Asia Minor, and this did not venture straight across the Ægean, because of his father's disaster, but went creeping round the northern coast. Mount Athos, standing out far and steep into the sea, stood in the way, and it was dangerous to go round it; so Xerxes thought it would be an undertaking worthy of him to have a canal dug across the neck that joins the mountain to the land, and the Greeks declared that he wrote a letter to the mountain god, bidding him not to put rocks in the way of the workmen of the "Great King." Traces of this canal can still be found in the ravine behind Mount Athos.

All the Greeks knew their danger now, and a council from every city met at the Isthmus of Corinth to consider what was to be done. All their ships, 271 in number, were gathered in a bay on the north of the great island of Eubœa. There the Spartan captain of the whole watched and waited, till beacons from height to height announced that the Persians were coming, and then he thought it safer to retreat within the Euripus, the channel between the island and the mainland, which is so narrow that a very few ships could stop the way of a whole fleet. However, just as they were within shelter, a terrible storm arose, which broke up and wrecked a great number of Persian ships, though the number that were left still was far beyond that of the Greeks. On two days the Greeks ventured out, and always gained the victory over such ships as they encountered, but were so much damaged themselves, without destroying anything like the whole fleet, that such fighting was hopeless work.

In the meantime Xerxes, with his monstrous land army, was marching on, and the only place where it seemed to the council at the Isthmus that he could be met and stopped was at a place in Thessaly, where the mountains of Œta rose up like a steep wall, leaving no opening but towards the sea, where a narrow road wound round the foot of the cliff, and between it and the sea was a marsh that men and horses could never cross. The springs that made this bog were hot, so that it was called Thermopylæ, or the Hot Gates.

The council at the Isthmus determined to send an army to stop the enemy there, if possible. There were 300 Spartans, and various troops from other cities, all under the command of one of the Spartan kings, Leonidas, who had married Gorgo, the girl whose word had kept her father faithful. They built up a stone wall in front of them, and waited for the enemy, and by-and-by the Persians came, spreading over an immense space in the rear, but in this narrow road only a few could fight at once, so that numbers were of little use. Xerxes sent to desire the Spartans to give up their arms. Leonidas only answered, "Come and take them." The Persian messenger reported that the Greeks were sitting on the wall combing their hair, while others were playing at warlike games. Xerxes thought they were mad, but a traitor Spartan whom he had in his camp said it was always the fashion of his countrymen before any very perilous battle. Xerxes made so sure of victory over such a handful of men, that he bade his captains bring them all alive to him; but day after day his best troops fell beaten back from the wall, and hardly a Greek was slain.

PASS OF THERMOPYLAE.

But, alas! there was a mountain path through the chestnut woods above. Leonidas had put a guard of Phocian soldiers to watch it, and the Persians did not know of it till a wretch, for the sake of reward, came and offered to show them the way, so that they might fall on the defenders of the pass from behind. In the stillness of the early dawn, the Phocians heard the trampling of a multitude on the dry chestnut leaves. They stood to arms, but as soon as the Persians shot their arrows at them they fled away and left the path open. Soon it was known in the camp that the foe were on the hills above. There was still time to retreat, and Leonidas sent off all the allies to save their lives; but he himself and his 300 Spartans, with 700 Thespians, would not leave their post, meaning to sell their lives as dearly as possible. The Delphic oracle had said that either Sparta or a king of Sparta must perish, and he was ready to give himself for his country. Two young cousins of the line of Hercules he tried to save, by telling them to bear his messages home; but one answered that he had come to fight, not carry letters, and the other that they would fight first, and then take home the news. Two more Spartans, whose eyes were diseased, were at the hot baths near. One went back with the allies, the other caused his Helot to lead him to the camp, where, in the evening, all made ready to die, and Leonidas sat down to his last meal, telling his friends that on the morrow they should sup with Pluto. One of these Thespians had answered, when he was told that the Persian arrows came so thickly as to hide the sky, "So much the better; we shall fight in the shade."

The Persians were by this time so much afraid of these brave men that they could only be driven against them by whips. Leonidas and his thousand burst out on them beyond the wall, and there fought the whole day, till everyone of them was slain, but with heaps upon heaps of dead Persians round them, so that, when Xerxes looked at the spot, he asked in horror whether all the Greeks were like these, and how many more Spartans there were. Like a barbarian, he had Leonidas' body hung on a cross; but in after times the brave king's bones were buried on the spot, and a mound raised over the other warriors, with the words engraven —

"Go, passer-by, at Sparta tell,
Obedient to her law, we fell."

There was nothing now between the Persians and the temple at Delphi. The priests asked the oracle if they should bury the treasures. "No," the answer was; "the god will protect his own." And just as a party of Persians were climbing up the heights to the magnificent temple there was a tremendous storm; rocks, struck by lightning, rolled down, and the Persians fled in dismay; but it is said Xerxes sent one man to insult the heathen god, and that he was a Jew, and therefore had no fears, and came back safe.

Now that Thermopylæ was lost, there was no place fit to guard short of the Isthmus of Corinth, and the council decided to build a wall across that, and defend it, so as to save the Peloponnesus. This left Attica outside, and the Athenians held anxious council what was to become of them. Before the way to Delphi was stopped, they had asked the oracle what they were to do, and the answer had been, "Pallas had prayed for her city, but it was doomed; yet a wooden wall should save her people, and at Salamis should women be made childless, at seed-time or harvest."

SALAMIS.

Themistocles said the wooden walls meant the ships, and that the Athenians were all to sail away and leave the city. Others would have it that the wooden walls were the old thorn fence of the Acropolis, and these, being mostly old people, chose to stay, while all the rest went away; and while the wives and children were kindly sheltered by their friends in the Peloponnesus, the men all joined the fleet, which lay off Salamis, and was now 366 in number. The Persians overran the whole country, overcame the few who held out the Acropolis, and set Athens on fire. All the hope of Greece was now in the fleet, which lay in the strait between Attica and the isle of Salamis. Eurybiades, the Spartan commander, still wanted not to fight, but Themistocles was resolved on the battle. Eurybiades did all he could to silence him. "Those who begin a race before the signal are scourged," said the Spartan. "True," said Themistocles; "but the laggards never win a crown." Eurybiades raised his leading staff as if to give him a blow. "Strike, but hear me," said Themistocles; and then he showed such good reason for there meeting the battle that Eurybiades gave way. Six days later the Persian fleet, in all its grandeur, came up, and Xerxes caused his throne to be set on Mount Ægaleos, above the strait, that he might see the battle. The doubts of the Peloponnesians revived. They wanted to sail away and guard their own shores, but Themistocles was so resolved that they should fight that he sent a slave with a message to Xerxes, pretending to be a traitor, and advising him to send ships to stop up the other end of the strait, to cut off their retreat. This was done, to the horror of honest Aristides, who, still exiled, was in Ægina, watching what to do for his countrymen. In a little boat he made his way at night to the ship where council was being held, and begged that Themistocles might be called out. "Let us be rivals still," he said; "but let our strife be which can serve our country best. I come to say that your retreat is cut off. We are surrounded, and must fight." Themistocles said it was the best thing that could happen, and led him into the council with his tidings.

They did fight. Ship was dashed against ship as fast as oars could bring them, their pointed beaks bearing one another down. The women who were made childless were Persian women. Two hundred Persian ships were sunk, and only forty Greek ones; an immense number were taken; and Xerxes, from his throne, saw such utter ruin of all his hopes and plans, that he gave up all thought of anything but getting his land army back to the Hellespont as fast as possible, for his fleet was gone!

## CHAP. XVIII. — THE BATTLE OF PLATÆA. b.c. 479-460.

After being thus beaten by sea, and having learnt what Greeks were by land, Xerxes himself, with a broken, sick, and distressed army, went back to Sardis; but he left a satrap named Mardonius behind him, with his best troops, in Thessaly, to see whether anything could still be done for his cause. He did try whether the Athenians could be persuaded to desert the other Greeks, and become allies of Persia, but they made a noble answer — "So long as the sun held his course, the Athenians would never be friends to Xerxes. Great as might be his power, Athens trusted to the aid of the gods and heroes, whose temple he had burnt."

After this answer, Mardonius marched again into Attica, and took possession of it; but as the Athenians were now all safe in Salamis, or among their friends, he could not do them much harm; and while he was finishing the ruin he had begun ten months before, the Spartans had raised their army, under the command of their king, Pausanias, nephew to Leonidas, and all the best soldiers from the other Greek cities. They came up with the Persians near the city of Platæa. Though a Spartan, Pausanias had rather not have fought; but when at last the battle began, it was a grand victory, and was gained in a wonderfully short time. The Spartans killed Mardonius, and put the best Persian troops, called the Immortals, to flight; and the Athenians, under Aristides, fought with the Thebans, who had joined the Persian army. The whole Persian camp was sacked. The Helots were sent to collect the spoil, and put it all together. They stole a good deal of the gold, which they took for brass, and sold it as such. Waggon-loads of silver and gold vessels were to be seen; collars, bracelets, and rich armour; and the manger of Xerxes' horses, which he had left behind, and which was of finely-worked brass. Pausanias bade the slaves of Mardonius to prepare such a feast as their master was used to, and then called his friends to see how useless were all the carpets, cushions, curtains, gold and silver, and the dainties upon them, and how absurd it was to set out on a conquering expedition thus encumbered.

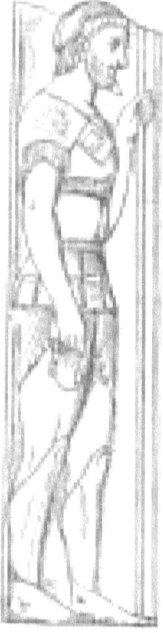

PRIAM SOLDIER

A tenth part of the spoil was set apart for Apollo, and formed into a golden tripod, supported by a brazen serpent with three heads. A great statue of Jupiter was sent to Olympia, the pedestal adorned with the names of all the cities which had sent men to the battle, and such another of Neptune was set up on the Isthmus; while a temple to Athene, adorned with pictures of the battle, was built on the spot near Platæa. Pausanias received a sample of all that was best of the spoil. Among the dead was found that one Spartan who had missed Thermopylæ. He had been miserable ever since, and only longed to die in battle, as now he had done. The Platæans were to be respected by all the other states of Greece, so long as they yearly performed funeral rites in honour of the brave men whose tombs were left in their charge.

TOMBS AT PLATAEA.

On the same day as the battle of Platæa was fought, another great battle was fought at Mykale, near Miletus, by the Ionian Greeks of Asia, assisted by Athenians and Spartans. It set Miletus free from the Persians, and was the first step backwards of their great power. The Athenian fleet also gained back the Chersonesus, and brought home the chains that had fastened together the bridge of boats, to be dedicated in the temples of their own gods.

The Athenians were all coming home rejoicing. Even the very week after Xerxes had burnt the Acropolis, the sacred olive which Pallas Athene was said to have given them had shot out a long branch from the stump, and now it was growing well, to their great joy and encouragement. Everyone began building up his own house; and Themistocles, Aristides, and the other statesmen prepared to build strong walls round the city, though the Spartans sent messengers to persuade them that it was of no use to have any fortified cities outside the Peloponnesus; but they knew this was only because the Spartans wanted to be masters of Greece, and would not attend to them. Athens stood about three miles from the coast, and in the port there had hitherto been a village called Piræus, and Themistocles persuaded the citizens to make this as strong as possible, with a wall of solid stone round it. These were grand days at Athens. They had noble architects and sculptors; and Æschylus was writing the grandest of his tragedies — especially one about the despair of the Persian women — but only fragments of most of them have come down to our time.

In 375 Aristides died, greatly honoured, though he was so poor that he did not leave enough to pay his funeral expenses; but a monument was raised to him by the State, and there is only one Athenian name as pure and noble as his.

The two other men who shared with him the honours of the defeat of the Persians met with very different fates, and by their own fault. When Pausanias went back to Sparta, he found his life there too stern and full of restraint, after what he had been used to in his campaign. He tried to break down the power of the Ephors, and obtain something more like royalty for the kings, and this he hoped to do by the help of Persia. He used to meet the messenger of this traitorous correspondence in the temple of Neptune, in the promontory of Tænarus. Some of the Ephors were warned, hid themselves there, and heard his treason from his own lips. They sent to arrest him as soon as he came back to Sparta; but he took refuge in the temple of Pallas, whence he could not be dragged. However, the Spartans were determined to have justice on him. They walled up the temple, so that he could neither escape nor have food brought to him; indeed it is said that, in horror at his treason, his mother brought the first stone. When he was at the point of death he was taken out, that the sanctuary might not be polluted, and he died just as he was carried out. The Spartans buried him close to the temple, and gave Pallas two statues of him, to make up for the suppliant she had lost, but they were always reproached for the sacrilege.

Themistocles was a friend of Pausanias, and was suspected of being mixed up in his plots. He was obliged to flee the country, and went to Epirus, where he came to the house of King Admetus, where the queen, Phthia, received him, and told him how to win her husband's protection, namely, by sitting down on the hearth by the altar to the household gods, and holding her little son in his arms.

When Admetus came in, Themistocles entreated him to have pity on his defenceless state. The king raised him up and promised his protection, and kept his word. Themistocles was taken by two guides safely across the mountains to Pydna, where he found a merchant ship about to sail for Asia. A storm drove it to the island of Naxos, which was besieged by an Athenian fleet; and Themistocles must have fallen into the hands of his fellow-citizens if he had landed, but he told the master of the ship that it would be the ruin of all alike if he were found in the vessel, and promised a large reward if he escaped. So the crew consented to beat about a whole day and night, and in the morning landed safely near Ephesus. He kept his word to the captain; for indeed he was very rich, having taken bribes, while Aristides remained in honourable poverty. He went to Susa, where Xerxes was dead; but the Persians had fancied his message before the battle of Salamis was really meant to serve them, and that he was suffering for his attachment to them, so the new king, Artaxerxes, the "Long-armed," who had a great esteem for his cleverness, was greatly delighted, offered up a sacrifice in his joy, and three times cried out in his sleep, "I have got Themistocles the Athenian."

Themistocles had asked to wait a year before seeing the king, that he might have time to learn the language. When he came, he put forward such schemes for conquering Greece that Artaxerxes was delighted, and gave him a Persian wife, and large estates on the banks of the Mæander, where he spent the rest of his life, very rich, but despised by all honest Greeks.

All the history of the war with Xerxes was written by Herodotus, a Greek of Caria, who travelled about to study the manners, customs, and histories of different nations, and recorded them in the most lively and spirited manner, so that he is often called the father of history.

Æschylus went on gaining prizes for his tragedies, till 468, when, after being thirteen times first, he was excelled by another Athenian named Sophocles, and was so much vexed that he withdrew to the Greek colonies in Sicily. It is not clear whether he ever came back to Athens for a time, but he certainly died in Sicily, and in an extraordinary way. He was asleep on the sea-shore, when an eagle flew above him with a tortoise in its claws. It is the custom of eagles to break the shells of these creatures by letting them fall on rocks from a great height. The bird took Æschylus' bald head for a stone, threw down the tortoise, broke his skull, and killed him!

Sophocles did not write such grand lines, yearning for the truth, as Æschylus, but his plays, of Ajax' madness, and especially of Antigone's self-devotion, were more touching, and full of human feeling; and Euripides, who was a little younger, wrote plays more like those of later times, with more of story in them, and more characters, especially of women. He even wrote one in which he represented Helen as never having been unfaithful at all; Venus only made up a cloud-image to be run away with by Paris, and Helen was carried away and hidden in Egypt, where Menelaus found her, and took her home. The works of these three great men have always been models. The Greeks knew their plays by heart almost as perfectly as the Iliad and Odyssey, and used to quote lines wherever they applied.

## CHAP. XIX. — THE AGE OF PERICLES. b.c. 464-429.

Athens and Sparta were now quite the greatest powers in Greece. No other state had dared to make head against the Persians, and all the lesser cities, and the isles and colonies, were anxious to obtain the help and friendship of one or other as their allies. The two states were always rivals, and never made common cause, except when the Persian enemy was before them. In the year 464 there was a terrible earthquake in Laconia, which left only five houses standing in Sparta, and buried great numbers in the ruins. The youths, who were all together in one building exercising themselves, were almost all killed by its fall; and the disaster would have been worse if the king, Archidamas, had not caused the trumpet to be blown, as if to call the people to arms, just outside the city. This brought all the men in order together just in time, for the Helots were rising against them, and, if they had found them groping each in the ruins of his house, might have killed them one by one; whereas, finding them up and armed, the slaves saw it was in vain, and dispersed.

The Messenians, who had never forgotten Aristodemus, hoped to free themselves again. A great many of the Helots joined them, and they made their fortified hill of Ithome very strong. The Spartans called on the Athenians to help them to put down the insurrection. The three greatest men in Athens were Pericles, the son of that Xanthippus who had impeached Miltiades; Kimôn, the son of Miltiades himself; and Ephialtes, a great orator, who was thought to be as upright as Aristides the Just. When the request from Sparta came, Ephialtes was against helping the rival of Athens; but Kimôn, who had friends in Laconia, declared that it would be unbecoming in Athens to let Greece be crippled in one of her two legs, or to lose her own yoke-fellow. He prevailed, and was sent with an army to help in the siege of Ithome; but it was such a tardy siege that the Spartans fancied that the Athenians had an understanding with the Messenians, and desired them to go home again, thus, of course, affronting them exceedingly.

Two years after, Kimôn was ostracised; but soon after the Spartans affronted the Athenians, by placing a troop of men at Tanagra, on the borders of Attica. The Athenians went out to attack them, and Kimôn sent to entreat permission to fight among his tribe, but he was not trusted, and was forbidden. He sent his armour to his friends — a hundred in number — and bade them maintain his honour. They were all killed, fighting bravely, and the victory was with the Spartans. Soon after, the virtuous Ephialtes was stabbed by some unknown person, and Pericles, feeling that good men could not be spared, moved that Kimôn should be called home again. Kimôn was much loved; he was tall and handsome, with curly hair and beard; and he was open-handed, leaving his orchards and gardens free to all, and keeping a table for every chance guest. Yet he much admired the Spartans and their discipline, and he contrived to bring about a five-years' truce between the two great powers. The greatest benefit he gave his people was the building of the Long Walls, which joined Athens and the Piræus together, so that the city could never be cut off from the harbour. Kimôn began them at his own expense, and Pericles persuaded the Athenians to go on with them, when their founder had been sent on an expedition to the isle of Cyprus, which was rising against the Persians. There Kimôn fell sick and died, but his fleet, immediately after, won a grand victory over the Phœnician and Cilician fleets, in the Persian service.

THE ACROPOLIS, ATHENS.

However, some hot-headed young Athenians were beaten at Coronea by the Bœotians, who were Spartan allies, and a good many small losses befel them by land, till they made another peace for thirty years in 445. There was nobody then in Athens, or Greece either, equal to Pericles, who was managing all affairs in his own city with great wisdom, and making it most beautiful with public buildings. On the rock of the Acropolis stood the Parthenon, the temple of the virgin goddess Pallas Athene, which was adorned with a portico, the remains of which still stand up gloriously against the blue Grecian sky. The bas-relief carvings on the pediments, representing the fight between the Centaurs and Lapithæ, are now in the British Museum; and though the statue itself is gone, still seals and gems remain, made to imitate it, and showing the perfect beauty of the ivory and gold statue of Athene herself, which was carved by the great sculptor Phidias, and placed within the temple. When there was a question whether this figure should be made of marble or of ivory, and Phidias recommended marble as the cheapest, the whole assembly of Athenians voted for ivory.

PROPYLAEA, ATHENS.

A beautiful fortification called the Propylæa guarded the west side of the Acropolis, where only there was no precipice; and there were other splendid buildings — a new open theatre, for the acting of those unrivalled tragedies of the three Athenian poets, and of others which have been lost; a Museum, which did not then mean a collection of curiosities, but a place where the youth might study all the arts sacred to the Muses; a Lyceum for their exercises, and schools for the philosophers. These schools were generally colonnades of pillars supporting roofs to give shelter from the sun, and under one of these taught the greatest, wisest, and best of all truth-seekers, namely, Socrates.

Though the houses at Athens stood irregularly on their steep hill, there was no place in the world equal to it for beauty in its buildings, its sculptures, and its carvings, and, it is also said, in its paintings; but none of these have come down to our times. Everything belonging to the Athenians was at this time full of simple, manly grace and beauty, and in both body and mind they were trying to work up to the greatest perfection they could devise, without any aid outside themselves to help them.

But they had come to the very crown of their glory. When a war arose between the Corinthians and the Corcyrans, who inhabited the isle now called Corfu, the Corcyrans asked to be made allies of Athens, and a fleet was sent to help them; and as the Corinthians held with Sparta, this brought on a great war between Athens and Sparta, which was called the Peloponnesian war, and lasted thirty years. It was really to decide which of the two great cities should be chief, and both were equally determined.

As Attica had borders open to the enemy, Pericles advised all the people in the country to move into the town. They sent their flocks into the isle of Eubœa, brought their other goods with them, and left their beautiful farms and gardens to be ravaged by the enemy; while the crowd found dwellings in a place under the west side of the Acropolis rock, which had hitherto been left empty, because an oracle declared it "better untrodden." Such numbers coming within the walls could not be healthy, and a deadly plague began to prevail, which did Athens as much harm as the war. In the meantime, Pericles, who was always cautious, persuaded the people to be patient, and not to risk battles by land, where the Spartans fought as well as they did, whereas nobody was their equal by sea; and as their fleet and all their many isles could save them from hunger, they could wear out their enemies, and be fresh themselves; but it was hard to have plague within and Spartans wasting their homes and fields without. Brave little Platæa, too, was closely besieged. All the useless persons had been sent to Athens, and there were only 400 Platæan and 80 Athenian men in it, and 110 women to wait on them; and the Spartans blockaded these, and tried to starve them out, until, after more than a year of famine, 220 of them scrambled over the walls on a dark, wet night, cut their way through the Spartan camp, and safely reached Athens. The other 200 had thought the attempt so desperate, that they sent in the morning to beg leave to bury the corpses of their comrades; but they then heard that only one man had fallen. They held out a few months longer, and then were all put to death, while the women were all made slaves. The children and the 220 were all made one with the Athenians.

Athens was in a piteous state from the sickness, which had cut off hosts of people of all ranks. It lasted seven or nine days in each, and seems to have been a malignant fever. Pericles lost his eldest son, his sister, and almost all his dearest friends in it; but still he went about calm, grave, and resolute, keeping up the hopes and patience of the

Athenians. Then his youngest and last son died of the same sickness, and when the time came for placing the funeral garland on his head, Pericles broke down, and wept and sobbed aloud. Shortly after, he fell sick himself, and lingered much longer than was usual with sufferers from the plague. Once, when his friends came in, he showed them a charm which the women had hung round his neck, and, smiling, asked them whether his enduring such folly did not show that he must be very ill indeed. Soon after, when he was sinking away, and they thought him insensible, they began to talk of the noble deeds he had done, his speeches, his wisdom and learning, and his buildings: "he had found Athens of brick," they said, "and had left her of marble." Suddenly the sick man raised himself in his bed, and said, "I wonder you praise these things in me. They were as much owing to fortune as to anything else; and yet you leave out what is my special honour, namely, that I never caused any fellow-citizen to put on mourning." So died this great man, in 429, the third year of the Peloponnesian war.

## CHAP. XX. — THE EXPEDITION TO SICILY. b.c. 415-413.

The Peloponnesian war went on much in the same way for some years after the death of Pericles. There was no such great man left in Athens. Socrates, the wise and deep-thinking philosopher, did not attend to state affairs more than was his duty as a citizen; and the leading man for some years was Nikias. He was an honest, upright man, but not clever, and afraid of everything new, so that he was not the person to help in time of strange dangers.

There was a youth growing up, however, of great ability. His name was Alkibiades. He was of high and noble family, but he had lost his parents very young, and Pericles had been his guardian, taking great care of his property, so that he was exceedingly rich. He was very beautiful in person, and that was thought of greatly at Athens, though he was laughed at for the pains he took to show off his beauty, and for carrying out to battle a shield inlaid with gold and ivory, representing Cupid hurling Jupiter's thunderbolts. His will was so determined, that, when he was a little boy at play in the street, and saw a waggon coming which would have spoiled his arrangements, he laid himself down before the wheels to stop it. He learnt easily, and, when he was with Socrates, would talk as well and wisely as any philosopher of them all; and Socrates really seems to have loved the bright, beautiful youth even more than his two graver and worthier pupils, Plato and Xenophon, perhaps because in one of Alkibiades' first battles, at Delium, he had been very badly wounded, and Socrates had carried him safely out of the battle on his broad shoulders. Socrates was very strong, but one of the ugliest of men, and the Athenians were amused at the contrast between master and pupil.

THE ACADEMIC GROVE, ATHENS.

But nobody could help loving Alkibiades in these early years, and he was a sort of spoiled child of the people. He won three crowns in the chariot races at the Olympic games, and feasted and made presents to his fellow-citizens afterwards, and he was always doing some strange thing in order to make a sensation. The first day that he was old enough to be admitted to the public assembly, while he was being greeted there, he let loose a tame quail, which he carried about under his cloak, and no business could be done till it had been caught. Another time he came very late, with a garland on his head, and desired to have the sitting put off because he had a feast at his house; and the grave archons actually granted his request. But the strangest thing he did was to cut off the tail of his beautiful dog, that, as he said, the Athenians might have something to talk about. In truth he made everything give way to his freaks and self-will; and he was a harsh and unkind husband, and insolent to his father-in-law; and, as time went on, he offended a great many persons by his pride and rudeness and selfishness, so that his brilliancy did little good.

There were Greek colonies in Sicily, but these were mostly in the interest of Sparta. There had been some fighting there in the earlier years of the war, and Alkibiades was very anxious to lead another expedition thither. Nikias thought this imprudent, and argued much against it; but the effect of his arguments was that the Athenians chose to join him in the command of it with Alkibiades, much against his will, for he was elderly, and out of health, and, of all men in Athens, he most disliked and distrusted Alkibiades.

Just as the fleet for Sicily was nearly ready, all the busts of Mercury which stood as mile-stones on the roads in Attica were found broken and defaced; and the enemies of Alkibiades declared that it was done in one of his drunken frolics. Such a thing, done to the figure of a god was not mere mischief, but sacrilege, and there was to be a great inquiry into it. Alkibiades wanted much to have the trial over before he sailed, that he might clear himself of the suspicion; and, indeed, it seems certain that whatever follies he might commit when he had nothing to do, he had then far too much to think of to be likely to bring himself into trouble by such a wanton outrage. But the Athenians chose to put off the inquiry till he was gone, and the fleet set sail — the largest that had ever gone from the Piræus — with sound of trumpet, libations poured into the sea from gold and silver bowls, songs and solemn prayers, as the 100 war galleys rowed out of the harbour in one long column. At Corcyra the fleet halted to meet their allies, who raised the number of ships to 154, containing 5000 heavily-armed men, with whom they made sail for Rhegium, the Italian foreland nearest to Sicily, whence they sent to make inquiries. They found more of the Greek cities were against them than they had expected, and their friends were weaker. Nikias wanted merely to sail round the island, and show the power of Athens, and then go home again. Lamachus, another general, wanted to make a bold attack on Syracuse at once; and Alkibiades had a middle plan, namely, to try to gain the lesser towns by force or friendship, and to stir up the native Sicels to revolt. This plan was accepted, and was going on well — for Alkibiades could always talk anyone over, especially strangers, to whom his gracefulness and brilliancy were new — when orders came from Athens that he and his friends were to be at once sent home from the army, to answer for the mischief done to the busts, and for many other crimes of sacrilege, which were supposed to be part of a deep plot for upsetting the laws of Solon, and making himself the tyrant of Athens.

This was, of course, the work of his enemies, and the very thing he had feared. His friends wrote to him that the people were so furious against him that he had no chance of a fair trial, and he therefore escaped on the way home, when, on his failing to arrive, he was solemnly cursed, and condemned to death. He took refuge in Sparta, where, fine gentleman as he was, he followed the rough, hardy Spartan manners to perfection, appeared to relish the black broth, and spoke the Doric Greek of Laconia, as it was said, more perfectly than the Spartans themselves. Unlike Aristides, and like the worse sort of exiles, he tried to get his revenge by persuading the allies of Athens in Asia Minor to revolt; and when the Spartans showed distrust of him, he took refuge with the Persian satrap Tissaphernes.

In the meantime, after he had left Sicily, Nikias was so cautious that the Syracusans thought him cowardly, and provoked a battle with him close to their own walls. He defeated them, besieged their city, and had almost taken it, when a Spartan and Corinthian fleet, headed by Gylippus, came out, forced their way through the Athenians, and brought relief to the city. More reinforcements came out to Athens, and there was a great sea-fight in front of the harbour at Syracuse, which ended in the total and miserable defeat of the Athenians, so that the army was obliged to retreat from Syracuse, and give up the siege. They had no food, nor any means of getting home, and all they could do was to make their way back into the part of the island that was friendly to them. Gylippus and the Syracusans tried to block their way, but old Nikias showed himself firm and undaunted in the face of misfortune, and they forced their way on for three or four days, in great suffering from hunger and thirst, till at last they were all hemmed into a small hollow valley, shut in by rocks, where the Syracusans shot them down as they came to drink at the stream, so thirsty that they seemed not to care to die so long as they could drink. Upon this, Nikias thought it best to offer to lay down his arms and surrender. All the remnant of the army were enclosed in a great quarry at Epipolæ, the sides of which were 100 feet high, and fed on a scanty allowance of bread and water, while the victors considered what was to be done with them, for in these heathen times there was no law of mercy for a captive, however bravely he might have fought. Gylippus wanted to save Nikias, for the pleasure of showing off so noble a prisoner at Sparta; but some of the Syracusans, who had been on the point of betraying their city to him, were afraid that their treason would be known, and urged that he should be put to death with his fellow-general; and the brave, honest, upright old man was therefore slain with his companion Demosthenes.

For seventy days the rest remained in the dismal quarry, scorched by the sun, half-starved, and rapidly dying off, until they were publicly sold as slaves, when many of the Athenians gained the favour of their masters by entertaining them by repeating the poetry of their tragedians, especially of Euripides, whose works had not yet been acted in Sicily. Some actually thus gained their freedom from their masters, and could return to Athens to thank the poet whose verses, stored in their memory, had been their ransom.

All the history of the Peloponnesian war is written by Thukydides, himself a brave Athenian soldier and statesman, who had a great share in all the affairs of the time, and well knew all the men whom he describes.

## CHAP. XXI. — THE SHORE OF THE GOAT'S RIVER. b.c. 406–402.

Still the war went on, the Athenians holding out steadily, but the Spartans beginning to care more for leadership than for Greece, and so making league with the Persians. Alkibiades was forgiven and called back again after a time, and he gained numerous towns and islands back again for the Athenians, so that he sailed into the Piræus with a fleet, made up by his own ships and prizes to full two hundred sail, all decked with purple, gold, and silver, and doubling what had been lost in the unhappy Sicilian enterprise; but his friends were sorry that it was what they called an unlucky day — namely, that on which every year the statue of Pallas Athene was stripped of its ornaments to be dusted, washed, and repaired, and on which her worshippers always avoided beginning anything or doing any business.

A very able man named Lysander, of the royal line, though not a king, had come into command at Sparta, and he had a sea-fight at Notium, just opposite to Ephesus, with the Athenians, and gained no very great advantage, but enough to make the discontent and distrust always felt for Alkibiades break out again, so that he was removed from the command and sailed away to the Chersonese, where in the time of his exile he had built himself a sort of little castle looking out on the strait.

Konon was the name of the next commander of the fleet, which consisted of 110 ships, with which he met the Spartan Kallikratidas with only fifty, near the three little islets called Arginusæ, near Malea. The numbers were so unequal that the Spartan was advised not to fight, but he answered that "his death would not hurt Sparta, but dishonour would hurt him." The Athenians gained a complete victory, Kallikratidas was killed, and the whole Spartan fleet broken up; but the Athenian fleet lost a great many men by a violent storm, which hindered the vessels from coming to the aid of those which had been disabled, and which therefore sunk in the tempest.

The relations of the men who had been drowned called for a trial of the commanders for neglecting to save the lives of their fellow-citizens, and there was such a bad spirit of party feeling in Athens at the time that they were actually condemned to death, all except Konon, though happily they were out of reach, and their sentence could not be executed. Lysander was, in the meantime, hard at work to collect a fresh fleet from the Spartan allies and to build new ships, for which he obtained money from the Persians at Sardis, where the satrap at that time was Cyrus, the son of Darius, the Great King, a clever prince, who understood something of Greek courage, and saw that the best thing for Persia was to keep the Greeks fighting with one another, so that no one state should be mightiest, or able to meddle with the Persian domains in Asia Minor. He gave Lysander the means of adding to his forces, and with his new fleet he plundered the shores of the islands of Salamis and Eubœa, and even of Attica itself, to insult the Athenians. Their fleet came out to drive him off. It had just been agreed by the Athenians that every prisoner they might take in the fight they expected should have his right thumb cut off, to punish the Greeks who had taken Persian gold. Lysander sailed away, with the Athenian fleet pursuing him up to the Hellespont, where he took the city of Lampsacus and plundered it before they came up, and anchored at a place called Ægos Potami, or the Goat's River, about two miles from Sestos. In the morning Lysander made all his men eat their first meal and then go on board, but gave orders that no ship should stir from its place. The Athenians too embarked, rowed up to Lampsacus and defied them; but as no Spartan vessel moved, they went back again to their anchorage, a mere open shore where there were no houses, so that all the crews went off to Sestos, or in search of villages inland, to buy provisions. The very same thing happened the next day. The challenge was not accepted by the Spartans, and the Athenians thought them afraid, grew more careless, and went further away from their ships. But on the hills above stood the little castle of Alkibiades, who could look down on the strait, see both fleets, and perceive that the Spartans sent swift galleys out each day to steal after the Athenians, so that they would be quite sure to take advantage of their foolish security. He could not bear to see his fellow-citizens ruining themselves, and came down to warn them and beg them to move into Sestos, where they would have the harbour to shelter them and the city behind them; but the generals scoffed at him, and bade him remember that they were commanders now, not he, and he went back to his castle, knowing only too well what would happen.

Till the fifth day all went on as before, but then Lysander ordered his watching galley to hoist a shield as a signal as soon as the Athenians had all gone off to roam the country in search of food, and then he spread out his fleet to its utmost width, and came rowing out with his 180 ships to fall upon the deserted Athenians. Not one general was at his post, except Konon, and he, with the eight galleys he could man in haste, sailed out in all haste — not to fight, for that was of no use, but to escape. Almost every vessel was found empty by the Spartans, taken or burnt, and then all the men were sought one by one as they were scattered over the country, except the few who were near enough to take refuge in the fort of Alkibiades. Out of the eight ships that got away, one went straight to Athens to carry the dreadful news; but Konon took the other seven with him to the island of Cyprus, thinking that thus he could do better for his country than share the ruin that now must come upon her.

It was night when the solitary ship reached the Piræus with the dreadful tidings; but they seemed to rush through the city, for everywhere there broke out a sound of weeping and wailing for husbands, fathers, brothers, and kinsmen lost, and men met together in the market-places to mourn and consult what could be done next. None went to rest that night; but the fleet was gone, and all their best men with it, and Lysander was coming down on Athens, putting down all her friends in the islands by the way, and driving the Athenian garrisons on before him into Athens. Before long he was at the mouth of the Piræus himself with his 150 galleys, and while he shut the Athenians in by sea, the Spartan army and its allies blockaded them by land.

If they held out, there was no hope of help; delay would only make the conquerors more bitter; so they offered to make terms, and very hard these were. The Athenians were to pull down a mile on each side of the Long Walls, give up all their ships except twelve, recall all their banished men, and follow the fortunes of the Spartans. They were very unwilling to accept these conditions, but their distress compelled them; and Lysander had the Long Walls pulled down to the sound of music on the anniversary of the day of the battle of Salamis. Then he overthrew the old constitution of Solon, and set up a government of thirty men, who were to keep the Athenians under the

Spartan yoke, and who were so cruel and oppressive that they were known afterwards as the thirty tyrants. So in 404 ended the Peloponnesian war, after lasting twenty-seven years.

The Athenians were most miserable, and began to think whether Alkibiades would deliver them, and the Spartans seem to have feared the same. He did not think himself safe in Europe after the ruin at Ægos Potami, and had gone to the Persian governor on the Phrygian coast, who received him kindly, but was believed to have taken the pay of either the Spartans or the thirty tyrants, to murder him, for one night the house where he was sleeping was set on fire, and on waking he found it surrounded with enemies. He wrapped his garment round his left arm, took his sword in his hand, and broke through the flame. None of the murderers durst come near him, but they threw darts and stones at him so thickly that at last he fell, and they despatched him. Timandra, the last of his wives, took up his body, wrapped it in her own mantle, and buried it in a city called Melissa. Such was the sad end of the spoilt child of Athens. He had left a son at Athens, whom the Thirty tried to destroy, but who escaped their fury, although during these evil times the Thirty actually put to death no less than fourteen hundred citizens of Athens, many of them without any proper trial, and drove five thousand more into banishment during the eight months that their power lasted. Then Thrasybulus and other exiles, coming home, helped to shake off their yoke and establish the old democracy; but even then Athens was in a weak, wretched state, and Sparta had all the power.

ATHENS.

## CHAP. XXII. — THE RETREAT OF THE TEN THOUSAND.
### b.c. 402–399.

Just as Greece was quieted by the end of the Peloponnesian war, the old King of Persia, Darius Nothus, died, and his eldest son, Artaxerxes Mnemon, came to the throne. He was the eldest, but his brother Cyrus, who had been born after his father began to reign, declared that this gave the best right, and resolved to march from Sardis into Persia to gain the kingdom for himself by the help of a hired body of Greek soldiers. Clearchus, a banished Spartan, undertook to get them together, and he made such descriptions of the wealth they would get in the East, that 11,000 of the bravest men in Greece came together for the purpose, and among them Xenophon, the pupil of Socrates, who has written the history of the expedition, as well as that of the later years of the Peloponnesian war. Xenophon was a horseman, but most of the troops were foot soldiers, and they were joined by a great body of Asiatics, raised by Cyrus himself. They were marched across Syria, crossed the present river Euphrates at the ford Thapsacus, and at Cunaxa, seven miles from Babylon, they met the enormous army which Artaxerxes had raised. The Greeks beat all who met them; but in the meantime Cyrus was killed, and his whole army broke up and fled, so that the Greeks were left to themselves in the enemy's country, without provisions, money, or guides.

BABYLON.

Artaxerxes sent messages pretending to wish to make terms with them and guide them safely back to their own country, provided they would do no harm on the way, and they willingly agreed to this, and let themselves be led where they were told it would be easier to find food for them; but this was across the great river Tigris, over a bridge of boats; and a few days after, Clearchus and the other chief officers were invited to the Persian camp to meet the king, and there seized and made prisoners. A message came directly after to the Greeks to bid them deliver up their arms, as they belonged to the Great King, having once belonged to his slave Cyrus.

To deliver up their arms was the last thing they intended; but their plight was dreadful — left alone eight months' march by the shortest way from home, with two great rivers and broad tracts of desert between it and themselves, and many nations, all hating them, in the inhabited land, with no guides, no generals, and ten times their number of Persian troops waiting to fall on them. All were in dismay;

hardly a fire was lighted to cook their supper; each man lay down to rest where he was, yet hardly anyone could sleep for fear and anxiety, looking for shame, death, or slavery, and never expecting to see Greece, wife, or children again.

But that night Xenophon made up his mind to do what he could to save his countrymen. The only hope was in some one taking the lead, and, as the Greeks had been true to their oaths throughout the whole march, he believed the gods would help them. So he called the chief of the officers still remaining together, and put them in mind that they might still hope. They were so much stronger and braver than the Persians, that if only they did not lose heart and separate, they could beat off almost any attack. As to provisions, they would seize them, and the rivers which they could not cross should be their guides, for they would track them up into the hills, where they would become shallow. Only every soldier must swear to assist in keeping up obedience, and then they would show Artaxerxes that, though he had seized Clearchus, they had ten thousand as good as he. The army listened, recovered hope and spirit, swore to all he asked, and one of the most wonderful marches in the world began. Cheirisophus, the eldest officer, a Spartan, took the command in the centre; Xenophon, as one of the youngest, was in the rear. They crossed the Zab, their first barrier, and then went upwards along the banks of the Tigris. The Persians hovered about them, and always attacked them every morning. Then the Greeks halted under any shelter near at hand, and fought them till towards evening. They were sure to fall back, as they were afraid to sleep near the Greeks, for fear of a night attack. Then the Greeks marched on for a good distance before halting to sup and sleep, and were able again to make a little way in the morning before the enemy attacked them again.

So they went on till they came to the mountains, where dwelt wild tribes whom the Great King called his subjects, but who did not obey him at all. However, they were robbers and very fierce, and stood on the steep heights shooting arrows and rolling down stones, so that the passage through their land cost the Greeks more men than all their march through Persia. On they went, through Armenia and over the mountains, generally having to fight their way, and, when they came very high up, suffering very much from the cold, and having to make their way through snow and ice, until at last, when they were climbing up Mount Theche, those behind heard a shout of joy, and the cry, "The sea, the sea!" rang from rank to rank. To every

Greek the sea was like home, and it seemed to them as if their troubles were over. They wept and embraced one another, and built up a pile of stones with a trophy of arms on the top, offering sacrifice to the gods for having so far brought them safely.

It was, however, only the Black Sea, the Pontus Euxinus, and far to the eastward; and, though the worst was over, they had still much to undergo while they were skirting the coast of Asia Minor. When they came to the first Greek colony — namely, Trapezus, or Trebizond — they had been a full year marching through an enemy's country; and yet out of the 11,000 who had fought at Cunaxa there were still 10,000 men safe and well, and they had saved all the women, slaves, and baggage they had taken with them. Moreover, though they came from many cities, and both Spartans and Athenians were among them, there never had been any quarrelling; and the only time when there had been the least dispute had been when Xenophon thought Cheirisophus a little too hasty in suspecting a native guide.

Tired out as the soldiers were, they wanted, as soon as they reached the Ægean Sea, to take ship and sail home; but they had no money, and the merchant ships would not give them a free passage, even if there had been ships enough, and Cheirisophus went to Byzantium to try to obtain some, while the others marched to wait for him at Cerasus, the place whence were brought the first cherries, which take their name from it. He failed, however, in getting any, and the Greeks had to make their way on; but they had much fallen away from the noble spirit they had shown at first. Any country that did not belong to Greeks they plundered, and they were growing careless as to whether the places in their way were Greek or not. Cheirisophus died of a fever, and Xenophon, though grieved at the change in the spirit of the army, continued for very pity in command. They hired themselves out to fight the battles of a Thracian prince, but, when his need of them was over, he dismissed them without any pay at all, and Xenophon was so poor that he was forced to sell the good horse that had carried him all the way from Armenia.

However, there was a spirited young king at Sparta, named Agesilaus, who was just old enough to come forward and take the command, and he was persuading his fellow-citizens, that now they had become the leading state in Greece, they ought to go and deliver the remaining Greek colonies in Asia Minor from the yoke of Persia, as Athens had done by the Ionians. They therefore decided on taking the remains of the 10,000 — now only 6000 — into their pay, and the messengers who came to engage them bought Xenophon's horse and restored it to him. Xenophon would not, however, continue with the band after he had conducted it to Pergamus, where they were to meet the Spartan general who was to take charge of them. On their way they plundered the house of a rich Persian, and gave a large share of the spoil to him as a token of gratitude for the wisdom and constancy that had carried them through so many trials.

It had been his strong sense of religion and trust in the care of the gods which had borne him up; and the first thing he did was to go and dedicate his armour and an offering of silver at the temple of Diana at Ephesus. This temple had grown up round a black stone image, very ugly, but which was said to have fallen from the sky, and was perhaps a meteoric stone. A white marble quarry near the city had furnished the materials for a temple so grand and beautiful that it was esteemed one of the seven wonders of the world.

After thus paying his vows, Xenophon returned to Athens, whence he had been absent two years and a-half. He not only wrote the history of this expedition, but a life of the first great Cyrus of Persia, which was meant not so much as real history, as a pattern of how kings ought to be bred up.

GREEK ARMOUR.

## CHAP. XXIII. — THE DEATH OF SOCRATES. b.c. 399.

Of the men who sought after God in the darkness, "if haply they might feel after Him," none had come so near the truth as Socrates, a sculptor by trade, and yet a great philosopher, and, so far as we can see, the wisest and best man who ever grew up without any guide but nature and conscience. Even the oracle at Delphi declared that he was the wisest of men, because he did not fancy he knew what he did not know, and did not profess to have any wisdom of his own. It was quite true — all his thinking had only made him quite sure that he knew nothing; but he was also sure that he had an inward voice within him, telling him which was the way in which he should walk. He did not think much about the wild tales of the Greek gods and goddesses; he seems to have considered them as fancies that had grown up on some forgotten truth, and he said a healthy mind would not dwell upon them; but he was quite sure that above all these there was one really true Most High God, who governed the world, rewarded the good, punished the bad, and sent him the inward voice, which he tried to obey to the utmost of his power, and by so doing, no doubt, his inward sight grew clearer and clearer. Even in his home his gentleness and patience were noted, so that when his scolding wife Xantippe, after railing at him sharply, threw some water at his head, he only smiled, and said, "After thunder follows rain." He did not open a school under a portico, but, as he did his work, all the choicest spirits of Greece resorted to him to argue out these questions in search of truth; and many accounts of these conversations have been preserved to us by his two best pupils, Plato and Xenophon.

SOCRATES.

But in the latter days of the Peloponnesian war, when the Athenians were full of bitterness, and had no great deeds to undertake outside their city, a foolish set of arguing pretenders to philosophy arose, who were called the Sophists, and who spent their time in mere empty talk, often against the gods; and the great Socrates was mixed up in people's fancy with them. A comic writer arose, named Aristophanes, who, seeing the Athenians fallen from the greatness of their fathers, tried to laugh them into shame at themselves. He particularly disliked Euripides, because his tragedies seemed, like the Sophists, not to respect the gods; and he also more justly hated Alkibiades for his overbearing ways, and his want of all real respect for gods or men. It was very hard on Socrates that the faults of his pupils should be charged against him; but Aristophanes had set all Athens laughing by a comedy called "The Clouds," in which a good-for-nothing young man, evidently meant for␣Alkibiades, gets his father into debt by buying horses, and, under the teaching of Socrates, learns both to cheat his creditors and to treat respect for his father as a worn-out notion. The beauty and the lisp of Alkibiades were imitated so as to make it quite plain who was meant by the youth; and Socrates himself was evidently represented by an actor in a hideous comic mask, caricaturing the philosopher's snub nose and ugly features. The play ended by the young man's father threatening to burn down the house of Socrates, with him in it. This had been written twenty years before, but it had been acted and admired again and again, together with the other comedies of Aristophanes — one about a colony of birds who try to build a city in the air, and of whom the chorus was composed; and another, called "The Frogs," still more droll, and all full of attacks on the Sophists.

Thus the Athenians had a general notion that Socrates was a corrupter of youth and a despiser of the gods, for in truth some forms of worship, like the orgies of Bacchus, and other still worse rites which had been brought in from the East, were such that no good man could approve them. One of the thirty tyrants had at one time been a pupil of his, and this added to the ill-feeling against him; and while Xenophon was still away in Asia, in the year 399, the philosopher was brought to trial on three points, namely, that he did not believe in the gods of Athens, that he brought in new gods, and that he misled young men; and for this his accusers demanded that he should be put to death.

Socrates pleaded his own cause before the council of the Areopagus. He flatly denied unbelief in the gods of his fathers, but he defended his belief in his genius or in-dwelling voice, and said that in this he was only like those who drew auguries from the notes of birds, thunder, and the like; and as for his guidance of young men, he called on his accusers to show whether he had ever led any man from virtue to vice. One of them answered that he knew those who obeyed and followed Socrates more than their own parents; to which he replied that such things sometimes happened in other matters — men consulted physicians about their health rather than their fathers, and obeyed their generals in war, not their fathers; and so in learning, they might follow him rather than their fathers. "Because I am thought to have some power of teaching youth, O my judges!" he ended, "is that a reason why I should suffer death? My accusers may procure that judgment, but hurt me they cannot. To fear death is to seem wise without being so, for it is pretending to understand what we know not. No man knows what death is, or whether it be not our greatest happiness; yet all fear and shun it."

His pupil Plato stood up on the platform to defend him, and began, "O ye Athenians, I am the youngest man who ever went up in this place — "

"No, no," they cried, with one voice; "the youngest who ever went down!" They would not hear a word from him; and 280 voices sentenced the great philosopher to die, after the Athenian fashion, by being poisoned with hemlock. He disdained to plead for a lessening of the penalty; but it could not be carried out at once, because a ship had just been sent to Delos with offerings, and for the thirty days while this was gone no one could be put to death. Socrates therefore was kept in prison, with chains upon his ankles; but all his friends were able to come and visit him, and one of them, named Krito, hoped to have contrived his escape by bribing the jailer, but he refused to make anyone guilty of a breach of the laws for the sake of a life which must be near its close, for he was not far from seventy years old; and when one of his friends began to weep at the thought of his dying innocent, "What!" he said, "would you think it better for me to die guilty?"

PLATO.

When the ship had come back, and the time was come, he called all his friends together for a cheerful feast, during which he discoursed to them as usual. All the words that fell from him were carefully stored up, and recorded by Plato in a dialogue, which is one of the most valuable things that have come down to us from Greek times. It was not Socrates, said the philosopher, whom they would lay in the grave. Socrates' better part, and true self, would be elsewhere;

and all of them felt sure that in that unknown world, as they told him, it must fare well with one like him. He begged them, for their own sakes, never to forget the lessons he had taught them; and when the time had come, he drank the hemlock as if it had been a cup of wine: he then walked up and down the room for a little while, bade his pupils remember that this was the real deliverance from all disease and impurity, and then, as the fatal sleep benumbed him, he lay down, bidding Krito not forget a vow he had made to one of the gods; and so he slept into death. "Thus," said Plato, "died the man who, of all with whom we were acquainted, was in death the noblest, in life the wisest and the best."

Plato himself carried on much of the teaching of his master, and became the founder of a sect of philosophy which taught that, come what may, virtue is that which should, above all, be sought for as making man noblest, and that no pain, loss, or grief should be shunned for virtue's sake. His followers were called Stoics, from their fashion of teaching in the porticos or porches, which in Greek were named stoai. Their great opponents were the Epicureans, or followers of a philosopher by name Epicurus, who held that as man's life is short, and as he knew not whence he came, nor whither he went, he had better make himself as happy as possible, and care for nothing else. Epicurus, indeed, declared that only virtue did make men happy; but there was nothing in his teaching to make them do anything but what pleased themselves, so his philosophy did harm, while that of the Stoics did good. A few Pythagoreans, who believed in the harmony of the universe, still remained; but as long as the world remained in darkness, thinking men were generally either Stoics or Epicureans.

## CHAP. XXIV. — THE SUPREMACY OF SPARTA. b.c. 396.

The ablest man just at this time in Greece was Agesilaus, one of the kings of Sparta. He was small, weakly, and lame, but full of courage, and an excellent general; and though he was as plain and hardy as suited with Spartan discipline, he had a warm, kind, tender heart, and was not ashamed to show it, as some of the Spartans were. So that, when some ambassadors came to see him, they found him riding on a stick to please his children; and again, when a trial of a distinguished man was going on in his absence, he wrote, "If he be not guilty, spare him for his own sake; if he be guilty, spare him for mine."

He was young, and full of fire and spirit, when the Spartans resolved to try to free the Greek colonies in Asia Minor from the Persians, by an army under his command. Xenophon had been so much grieved by his master Socrates' death that he would not remain at Athens, but joined his old friends once more, and was a great friend of Agesilaus. The Athenians, Corinthians, and Thebans were all asked to send troops, but they refused, and Agesilaus set sail with 8000 men, meaning to meet and take with him the remains of the 10,000, who were well used to warfare with the Persians. He was the first Greek king who had sailed to Asia since the Trojan war, and, in imitation of Agamemnon, he stopped at Aulis, in Bœotia, to offer sacrifice to Diana. He dreamt that a message came that it ought to be the same sacrifice as Agamemnon had made, but he declared that he would not act so cruelly towards his own child, and caused a white hind to be crowned, and offered as the goddess' chosen offering; but as this was not the usual sacrifice, the Thebans were affronted, and threw away the sacrifice as it lay on the altar. This was reckoned as a bad omen, and Agesilaus went on his way, doubting whether he should meet with success.

He was a man who went very much by omens, for after he had landed, had gained several successes, and was just advancing into Caria, at the sacrifice he found the liver of one of the victims imperfect, and this decided him on going back to Ephesus for the winter, to collect more horse. When he marched on in the spring he was much stronger; he advanced into the Persian territories, and defeated the Persians and their allies wherever he met them, and at last the satrap Pharnabazus begged to have a conference with him, being much struck with his valour.

Agesilaus came first to the place of meeting, and having to wait there, sat down on the grass under a tree, and began to eat his homely meal of bread and an onion. Presently up came the satrap in all his splendour, with attendants carrying an umbrella over his head, and others bearing rich carpets and costly furs for him to sit on, silver and gold plate, and rich food and wines. But when he found that the little, shabby, plain man under the tree was really the mighty king of Sparta, the descendant of Hercules, Pharnabazus was ashamed of all his pomp, and went down upon the ground by Agesilaus' side, to the great damage, as the Greeks delighted to observe, of his fine, delicately-tinted robes. He told Agesilaus that he thought this attack a bad reward for all the help that the Spartans had had from Persia in the Peloponnesian war; but Agesilaus said that they had been friends then, but that as cause of war had arisen it was needful to fight, though he was so far from feeling enmity that Pharnabazus should find the Greeks willing to welcome him, and give him high command, if he would come and be a free man among them. Pharnabazus answered that as long as he held command in the name of the Great King he must be at war with the foes of Persia, but if Artaxerxes should take away his satrapy he would come over to the Spartans. Therewith Agesilaus shook hands with him, and said, "How much rather I would have so gallant a man for my friend than my enemy?" The young son of the satrap was even more taken with the Spartan, and, waiting behind his father, ran up to the king, and, according to the Persian offer of friendship, said, "I make you my guest," at the same time giving him a javelin. Agesilaus looked about for anything fine enough to offer the young Persian in return, and seeing that a youth in his train had a horse with handsome trappings, asked for them, and made a gift of them to his new friend. The friendship stood the youth in good stead, for when he was afterwards driven from home by his brethren, Agesilaus welcomed him in Laconia, and was very kind to him. The war, however, still continued, and Agesilaus gained such successes that the Persians saw their best hope lay in getting him recalled to Greece; so they sent money in secret to the Athenians and their old allies to incite them to revolt, and so strong an army was brought together that the Spartans sent in haste to recall Agesilaus. The summons came just as he was mustering all the Greek warriors in Asia Minor for an advance into the heart of the empire, and he was much disappointed; but he laughed, and, as Persian coins were stamped with the figure of a horseman drawing the bow, he said he had been defeated by 10,000 Persian archers.

He marched home by the way of the Hellespont, but before he was past Thrace a great battle had been fought close to Corinth, in which the Spartans had been victorious and made a great slaughter of the allies. But he only thought of them as Greeks, not as enemies, and exclaimed, "O Greece, how many brave men hast thou lost, who might have conquered all Persia!" The Thebans had joined the allies against Sparta, and the Ephors sent orders to Agesilaus to punish them on his way southwards. This he did in the battle of Coronea, in which he was very badly wounded, but, after the victory was over, he would not be taken to his tent till he had been carried round the field to see that every slain Spartan was carried away in his armour and not left to the plunderers.

He then returned to Sparta, where the citizens were delighted to see that he had not been spoiled by Persian luxury, but lived as plainly as ever, and would not let his family dress differently from others. He knew what greatness was so well, that when he heard Artaxerxes called the Great King, he said, "How is he greater than I, unless he be the juster?"

It should be remembered that Konon, that Athenian captain who had escaped from Ægos Potami with six ships, had gone to the island of Cyprus. He persuaded the people of the island of Rhodes to revolt from the Spartans, and make friends with the Persians. It is even said that he went to the court of Artaxerxes, and obtained leave from him to raise ships, with which to attack the Spartans, from the colonies which were friendly to Athens, yet belonged to the Greek Empire. Pharnabazus joined him, and, with eighty-five ships, they cruised about in the Ægean Sea, and near Cnidus they entirely defeated the Spartan fleet. It was commanded by Pisander, Agesilaus' brother-in-law, who held by his ship to the last, and died like a true Spartan, sword in hand.

After this Konon drove out many Spartan governors from the islands of the Ægean, and, sailing to Corinth, encouraged the citizens to hold out against Sparta, after which Pharnabazus went home, but Konon returned with the fleet to the Piræus, and brought money and aid to build up the Long Walls again, after they had been ten years in ruins. The crews of the ships and the citizens of Athens all worked hard, the rejoicing was immense, and Konon was looked on as the great hero and benefactor of Athens; but, as usual, before long the Athenians grew jealous of him and drove him out, so that he ended his life an exile, most likely in Cyprus.

It was no wonder that Xenophon's heart turned against the city that thus treated her great men, though he ought not to have actually fought against her, as he did under Agesilaus, whom he greatly loved. The chief scene of the war was round Corinth; but at last both parties were wearied, and a peace was made between Athens and Sparta and the Persian Empire. Artaxerxes kept all the Greek cities in Asia and the islands of Cyprus and Clazomene, and all the other isles and colonies were declared free from the power of any city, except the isles of Lemnos, Imbros, and Scyros, which were still to belong to Athens. Sparta required of Thebes to give up her power over the lesser cities of Bœotia, but Sparta herself did not give up Messenia and the other districts in the Peloponnesus, so that she still remained the strongest. This was called the peace of Antaleidas.

Xenophon did not go back to Athens, but settled on a farm near Elis, where he built a little temple to Diana, in imitation of the one at Ephesus, and spent his time in husbandry, in hunting, and in writing his histories, and also treatises on dogs and horses. Once a-year he held a great festival in honour of Diana, offering her the tithe of all his produce, and feasting all the villagers around on barley meal, wheaten bread, meat, and venison, the last of which was obtained at a great hunting match conducted by Xenophon himself and his sons.

VIEW ON THE EUROTAS IN LACONIA.

## CHAP. XXV. — THE TWO THEBAN FRIENDS. b.c. 387–362.

By the peace of Antaleidas things had been so settled that the Spartans had the chief power over Greece, and they used it in their proud, harsh way. In the year 387 they called the Thebans to assist in besieging the city of Mantinea, in a valley between Argos and Arcadia. The Mantineans sallied out, and there was a battle, in which they were defeated; but in the course of it a Theban youth of a rich and noble family, named Pelopidas, was surrounded by enemies. He fought desperately, and only fell at last under seven wounds just as another Theban, a little older, named Epaminondas, broke into his rescue, and fought over him until the Spartans made in and bore them off, but not till Epaminondas had likewise been badly wounded. He was the son of a poor but noble father, said to be descended from one of the men who had sprung from the dragon's teeth; and he had been well taught, and was an earnest philosopher of the Pythagorean school, striving to the utmost of his power to live a good and virtuous life. A close friendship grew up between him and Pelopidas, though the one loved books, and the other, dogs and horses; but Pelopidas tried to be as upright and noble as his friend, and, though a very rich man, lived as hardily and sparingly as did Epaminondas, using his wealth to help the poor. When some foolish friends asked him why he did not use his riches for his own ease and pomp, he laughed at them, and, pointing to a helpless cripple, said that riches were only useful to a man like that.

Every high-spirited Theban hated the power that Sparta had taken over their free state, and wanted to shake it off; but some of those who were bribed by Sparta sent word of their intentions to a Spartan general in the neighbourhood, whereupon he came down on Thebes in the middle of a festival, seized the citadel called the Cadmea, put in a Spartan garrison, and drove 300 of the best Thebans into exile. Pelopidas was among them, while Epaminondas was thought of only as a poor student, and was unnoticed; but he went quietly on advising the Theban young men to share the warlike exercises of the Spartans in the Cadmea, so as to get themselves trained to arms in case there should be a chance of fighting for their freedom. In the fourth year of the exile, Pelopidas wrote to beg his friend to join in a plot by which some of the banished were to creep into the city, go to a banquet that was to be given to the chief friends of the Spartans disguised as women, kill them, proclaim liberty, raise the citizens, and expel the Spartans. But Epaminondas would have nothing to do with a scheme that involved falsehood and treachery, however much he longed to see his country free. But on a dark, winter evening, Pelopidas and eleven more young exiles came one by one into Thebes, in the disguise of hunters, and met at the house of the friend who was going to give the feast. They were there dressed in robes and veils, and in the height of the mirth the host brought them in, and they fell upon the half-tipsy guests and slew them, while Pelopidas had gone to the house of the most brave and sober among them, challenged him, and killed him in fair fight. Then they shouted, "Freedom! Down with the foe!" The citizens rose, Epaminondas among the first; the rest of the exiles marched in at daybreak, and the Cadmea was besieged until the Spartans were obliged to march out, and Thebes was left to its own government by Bœotarchs, or rulers of Bœotia, for a year at a time, of whom Pelopidas was at once chosen to be one.

Of course there was a war, in which the Thebans were helped by Athens, but more from hatred to Sparta than love to Thebes. After six years there was a conference to arrange for a peace, and Epaminondas, who was then Bœotarch, spoke so well as to amaze all hearers. Agesilaus demanded that the Thebans should only make terms for themselves, and give up the rest of Bœotia, and Epaminondas would not consent unless in like manner Sparta gave up the rule over the other places in Laconia. The Athenians would not stand by the Thebans, and all the allies made peace, so that Thebes was left alone to resist Sparta, and Epaminondas had to hurry home to warn her to defend herself.

The only thing in favour of Thebes was that Agesilaus' lame leg had become so diseased that he could not for five years go out to war; but the other king, Cleombrotus, was at the head of 11,000 men marching into Bœotia, and Epaminondas could only get together 6000, with whom he met them at Leuctra. No one doubted how the battle would end, for the Spartans had never yet been beaten, even by the Athenians, when they had the larger numbers, and, besides, the quiet scholar Epaminondas had never been thought of as a captain. The omens went against the Thebans, but he said he knew no token that ought to forbid a man from fighting for his country. Pelopidas commanded the horsemen, and Epaminondas drew up his troop in a column fifty men deep, with which he dashed at the middle of the Spartan army, which was only three lines deep, and Pelopidas' cavalry hovered about to cut them down when they were broken. The plan succeeded perfectly. Cleombrotus was carried dying from the field, and Epaminondas had won the most difficult victory ever yet gained by a Greek. So far from being uplifted by it, all he said was how glad he was that his old father and mother would be pleased. The victory had made Thebes the most powerful city in Greece, and he was the leading man in Thebes for some time; but he had enemies, who thought him too gentle with their foes, whether men or cities, and one year, in the absence of Pelopidas, they chose him to be inspector of the cleanliness of the streets, thinking to put a slur on him; but he fulfilled the duties of it so perfectly that he made the office itself an honourable one.

Pelopidas was soon after sent on a message to Alexander, the savage tyrant of Thessaly, who seized him and put him in chains in a dismal dungeon. The Theban army marched to deliver him, Epaminondas among them as a common soldier; but the two Bœotarchs in command managed so ill that they were beset by the Thessalian horsemen and forced to turn back. In the retreat they were half-starved, and fell into such danger and distress, that all cried out for Epaminondas to lead them, and he brought them out safely. The next year he was chosen Bœotarch, again attacked Thessaly, and, by the mere dread of his name, made the tyrant yield up Pelopidas, and beg for a truce. Pelopidas brought home such horrible accounts of the cruelties of Alexander, that as soon as the truce was over, 7000 men, with him at their head, invaded Thessaly, and won the battle of Cynocephalæ, or the Dogs' Heads. Here Pelopidas was killed, to the intense grief of the army, who cut their hair and their horses' manes and tails, lighted no fire, and tasted no food on that sad night after their victory, and great was the mourning at Thebes for the brave and upright man who had been thirteen times Bœotarch. Epaminondas was at sea with the fleet he had persuaded the Thebans to raise; but the next year he was sent into the Peloponnesus to defend the allies there against the

Spartans. He had almost taken the city itself, when the army hastened back to defend it, under the command of Agesilaus, who had recovered and taken the field again.

Close to Mantinea, where Epaminondas had fought his first battle, he had to fight again with the only general who had as yet a fame higher than his — namely, Agesilaus — and Xenophon was living near enough to watch the battle. It was a long, fiercely-fought combat, but at last the Spartans began to give way and broke their ranks, still, however, flinging javelins, one of which struck Epaminondas full in the breast, and broke as he fell, leaving a long piece of the shaft fixed in the wound. His friends carried him away up the hill-side, where he found breath to ask whether his shield were safe, and when it was held up to him, he looked down on the Spartans in full flight, and knew he had won the day. He was in great pain, and he was told that to draw out the spear would probably kill him at once. He said, therefore, that he must wait till he could speak to the two next in command; and when he was told that they were both slain, he said, "Then you must make peace," for he knew no one was left able to contend against Agesilaus. As his friends wept, he said, "This day is not the end of my life, but the beginning of my happiness and completion of my glory;" and when they bewailed that he had no child, he said, "Leuctra and Mantinea are daughters enough to keep my name alive." Then, as those who stood round faltered, unable to resolve to draw out the dart, he pulled it out himself with a firm hand, and the rush of blood that followed ended one of the most beautiful lives ever spent by one who was a law unto himself. He was buried where he died, and a pillar was raised over the spot bearing the figure of a dragon, in memory of his supposed dragon lineage.

THESSALONICA.

## CHAP. XXVI. — PHILIP OF MACEDON. b.c. 364.

Peace was made as Epaminondas desired, and Bœotia never produced another great man, as, indeed, the inhabitants had always been slow and dull, so that a Bœotian was a by-word for stupidity. The only other great Bœotian was the poet Pindar, who was living at this time.

The fifteen years of Theban power had weakened Sparta; but Agesilaus persuaded the Ephors to send him to assist Tachos, who had revolted from the Persians and made himself king of Egypt, and who promised to pay the Spartans well for their aid. When he sent his officers to receive the Spartan king who had achieved the greatest fame of any man then living, they absolutely burst out laughing at the sight of the little, lame man, now more than eighty years old, and as simply clad as ever; and he was much vexed and angered that he was not made commander of the army, but only of the foreign allies; and when Tachos went against his advice, and chose to march into Phœnicia, he went over to the cause of another Egyptian prince, a cousin to Tachos, named Nectanebes, whom he helped to gain the crown of Egypt, thus breaking his promises in a way which we are sorry should have been the last action of his long life. The next winter he embarked to return home, but he was driven by contrary winds to a place in Egypt called the port of Menelaus, because that king of Sparta had been so long weather-bound there. The storm had been too much for the tough old frame of Agesilaus, who died there. His body was embalmed in wax, and carried home to be buried at Sparta, whose greatest man he certainly was.

The great Persian Empire was growing weak, and her subject cities were revolting from her. Caria, in Asia Minor, became free under its king, Mausolus, who reigned twenty-four years, but who is chiefly famous for the magnificent monument which his widow Artemisia raised to his memory, and which consisted of several stages of pillars, supported by tablets so exquisitely sculptured that the Mausoleum, as it was called, was taken into the number of the seven wonders of the world. After all, its splendour did not comfort the heart of Artemisia, and she had the ashes of her husband taken from his urn and carried them about her in a casket, until finally she put them in water and drank them, so as to be for ever one with them. She was herself buried in the Mausoleum, the remains of which have lately been discovered, and are now placed in the British Museum.

One more great man had grown up in Athens — namely, Demosthenes. He was the son of an Athenian sword merchant, who died when he was but seven years old. His guardians neglected his property, and he was a sickly boy, with some defect in his speech, so that his mother kept him at home as much as she could, and he was never trained in mind or body like the other Athenian youth; but, as he grew older, he seems to have learned much from the philosopher Plato, and he set himself to lead the Athenians as a public speaker. For this he prepared himself diligently, putting pebbles in his mouth to overcome his stammering, and going out to make speeches to the roaring waves of the sea, that he might learn not to be daunted by the shouts of the raging people; and thus he taught himself to be the most famous orator in the world, just as Phidias was the greatest sculptor and Æschylus the chief tragedian.

DEMOSTHENES.

His most eloquent discourses are called Philippics, because they were against Philip, king of Macedon, a power that was growing very dangerous to the rest of Greece. It lay to the northward of the other states, and had never quite been reckoned as part of Greece, for a rough dialect that was spoken there, and the king had been forced to join the Persian army when Xerxes crossed his country; but he had loved the Greek cause, and had warned Aristides at the battle of Platæa. The royal family counted Hercules as their forefather, and were always longing to be accepted as thorough Greeks. One of the young princes, named Philip, was taken to Thebes by Pelopidas, to secure him from his enemies at home. He was lodged in the house of Epaminondas' father, and was much struck with the grand example he there beheld, though he cared more for the lessons of good policy he then learned than for those of virtue.

Two years after the battle of Mantinea, Philip heard that his elder brother, the king, was dead, leaving only a young infant upon the throne. He went home at once and took the guardianship of the kingdom, gained some great victories over the wild neighbours of Macedon, to the north, and then made himself king, but without hurting his nephew, who grew up quietly at his court, and by-and-by married one of his daughters. He had begun to train his troops to excellent discipline, perfecting what was called the Macedonian phalanx, a manner of arraying his forces which he had learned in part from Epaminondas. The phalanx was a body of heavily-armed foot soldiers, each carrying a shield, and a spear twenty-four feet long. When they advanced, they were taught to lock their shields together, so as to form a wall, and they stood in ranks, one behind the other, so that the front row had four spear points projecting before them.

He also made the Macedonian nobles send their sons to be trained to arms at his court, so as to form a guard of honour, who were comrades, friends, and officers to the king. In the meantime, wars were going on — one called the Social War and one the Sacred War — which wasted the strength of the Thebans, Spartans, and Athenians all alike, until Philip began to come forward, intending to have power over them all. At first, he marched into Thrace, the wild country to the north, and laid siege to Methone. In this city there was an archer, named Aster, who had once offered his service to the Macedonian army, when Philip, who cared the most for his phalanx, rejected him contemptuously, saying, "I will take you into my pay when I make war on starlings." This man shot an arrow, with the inscription on it, "To Philip's right eye;" and it actually hit the mark, and put out the eye. Philip caused it to be shot back again with the inscription, "If Philip takes the city, he will hang Aster." And so he did. Indeed he took the loss of his eye so much to heart, that he was angry if anyone mentioned a Cyclops in his presence.

After taking Methone, he was going to pass into Thessaly, but the Athenians held Thermopylæ, and he waited till he could ally himself with the Thebans against the Phocians. He took Phocis, and thus gained the famous pass, being able to attack it on both sides. Next he listened to envoys from Messenia and Argos, who complained of the dominion of the Spartans, and begged him to help them. The Athenians were on this urged by Demosthenes, in one of his Philippics, to forget all their old hatred to Sparta, and join her in keeping back the enemy of both alike; and their intention of joining Sparta made Philip wait, and begin by trying to take the great island of Euboea, which he called the "Shackles of Greece." To its aid was sent a body of Athenians, under the command of Phocion, a friend of Plato, and one of the sternest of Stoics, of whom it was said that no one had ever seen him laugh, weep, or go to the public baths. He went about barefoot, and never wrapped himself up if he could help it, so that it was a saying, "Phocion has got his cloak on; it is a hard winter." He was a great soldier, and, for the time, drove back the Macedonians from Euboea. But very few Athenians had the spirit of Phocion or Demosthenes. They had grown idle, and Philip was bribing all who would take his money among the other Greeks to let his power and influence spread, until at last he set forth to invade Greece. The Thebans and Athenians joined together to stop him, and met him at Chæronea, in Bœotia; but neither city could produce a real general, and though at first the Athenians gained some advantage, they did not make a proper use of it, so that Philip cried out, "The Athenians do not know how to conquer," and, making another attack, routed them entirely. Poor Demosthenes, who had never been in a battle before, and could only fight with his tongue, fled in such a fright that when a bramble caught his tunic, he screamed out, "Oh, spare my life!" The battle of Chæronea was a most terrible overthrow, and neither Athens nor Thebes ever recovered it. Macedon entirely gained the chief power over Greece, and Philip was the chief man in it, though Demosthenes never ceased to try to stir up opposition to him. Philip was a very able man, and had a good deal of nobleness in his nature. Once, after a feast, he had to hear a trial, and gave sentence in haste. "I appeal," said the woman who had lost. "Appeal? and to whom?" said the king. "I appeal from Philip drunk to Philip sober." He was greatly struck, heard the case over again the next day, and found that he had been wrong and the woman right.

## CHAP. XXVII. — THE YOUTH OF ALEXANDER. b.c. 356–334.

Philip of Macedon married Olympias, the daughter of the king of Epirus, who traced his descent up to Achilles. She was beautiful, but fierce and high-spirited; and the first time Philip saw her she was keeping the feast of Bacchus, and was dancing fearlessly among great serpents, which twisted about among the maidens' vine-wreathed staves, their baskets of figs, and even the ivy crowns on their heads. Her wild beauty charmed him, and he asked her in marriage as soon as he had gained the throne. The son of this marriage, Alexander, was born at Pella in 356. On the same day a great battle was won by Parmenio, Philip's chief general, and the king's horses won the prize at the Olympic games. Philip was so prosperous that he declared he must sacrifice to the gods, or they would be jealous, and cast him down in the midst of his happiness. That same night the wonder of the world, the temple of Diana at Ephesus, was burnt down by a madman named Erostratus, who thought the deed would make him for ever famous. It was built up again more splendidly than ever, and the image was saved.

DIANA OF EPHESUS.

The chief physician at Philip's court was Aristotle, a Macedonian of Stagyra, who had studied under Plato, and was one of the greatest and best of philosophers; and Philip wrote to him at once that he rejoiced not only in having a son, but in his having been born when he could have Aristotle for a tutor. For seven years, however, the boy was under the care of a noble lady named Lanika, whom he loved all his life, and then was placed with a master, who taught him to repeat the Iliad and Odyssey from end to end. He delighted in them so much that he always carried a copy about with him, and constantly dreamt of equalling his great forefather Achilles.

When he was about thirteen, a magnificent black horse called Bucephalus, or Bull-head, because it had a white mark like a bull's face on its forehead, was brought to Philip; but it was so strong and restive that nobody could manage it, and Philip was sending it away, when Alexander begged leave to try to tame it. First he turned its head to the sun, having perceived that its antics were caused by fear of its own shadow; then stroking and caressing it as he held the reins, he gently dropped his fluttering mantle and leaped on its back, sitting firm through all its leaps and bounds, but using neither whip nor spur nor angry voice, till at last the creature was brought to perfect obedience. This gentle courage and firmness so delighted Philip that he embraced the boy with tears of joy, and gave him the horse, which, as long as it lived, loved and served him like no one else. Philip also said that such a boy might be treated as a man, and therefore put him under Aristotle three years earlier than it was usual to begin philosophy; and again he was an apt and loving scholar, learning great wisdom in dealing with men and things, and, in truth, learning everything but how to control his temper.

At the battle of Chæronea, Alexander was old enough to command the division which fought against the Thebans, and entirely overthrew them; so that when peace was made, Sparta was the only city that refused to own the superior might of Macedon, and the Council of the States chose Philip as commander of the Greeks in the grand expedition he was going to undertake against Persia.

But Philip had eastern vices. He was tired of Olympias' pride and wilfulness, and took another wife, whom he raised to the position of queen; and at the banquet a half-tipsy kinsman of this woman insulted Alexander, who threw a cup at the man. Philip started up to chastise his son, but, between rage and wine, fell down, while Alexander said, "See, a man preparing to cross from Europe to Asia cannot step safely from one couch to another!"

Then he took his mother to her native home, and stayed away till his father sent for him, but kept him in a kind of disgrace, until at the wedding feast of Alexander's sister Cleopatra with the king of Epirus, just as Philip came forward in a white garment, a man darted forward and thrust a sword through his body, then fled so fast that he would have escaped if his foot had not been caught in some vine stocks, so that the guards cut him to pieces.

Alexander was proclaimed king, at only twenty years old; and Demosthenes was so delighted at the death of the enemy of Athens, that he wreathed his head with a garland in token of joy, little guessing that Philip's murder had only placed a far greater man on the throne. The first thing Alexander did was to go to Corinth, and get himself chosen in his father's stead captain-general of the Greeks. Only the Spartans refused, saying it was their custom to lead, and not to follow; while the Athenians pretended to submit, meaning to take the first opportunity of breaking off the yoke. Before Alexander could march, however, to Persia, he had to leave all safe behind him; so he turned northwards to subdue the wild tribes in Thrace. He was gone four months, and the Greeks heard nothing of him, so that the Thebans thought he must be lost, and proclaimed that they were free from the power of Macedon.

Their punishment was terrible. Alexander came back in haste, fought them in their own town, hunted them from street to street, killed or made slaves of all who had not been friends of his father, pulled down all the houses, and divided the lands between the other Bœotian cities. This was for the sake of making an example of terror; but he afterwards regretted this act, and, as Bacchus was the special god of Thebes, he thought himself punished by the fits of rage that seized him after any excess in wine. The other Greeks, all but the Spartans, again sent envoys to meet Alexander at Corinth, and granted him all the men, stores, and money he asked for. The only person who did not bow down to him was Diogenes, a philosopher who so exaggerated Stoicism that he was called the "Mad Socrates." His sect were called Cynics, from Cyon, a dog, because they lived like dogs, seldom washing, and sleeping in any hole. Diogenes' lair was a huge earthenware tub, that belonged to the temple of the mother of the gods, Cybele; and here Alexander went to see him, and found him basking in the sun before it, but not choosing to take any notice of the princely youth who addressed him — "I am Alexander the King."

"And I am Diogenes the Cynic," was the answer, in a tone as if he thought himself quite as good as the king. Alexander, however, talked much with him, and ended by asking if he could do anything for him.

"Only stand out of my sunshine," was the answer; and as the young king went away he said, "If I were not Alexander, I would be Diogenes;" meaning, perhaps, that if he were not to master all earthly things, he would rather despise them. Twelve years later, Diogenes, then past ninety, was found dead in his tub, having supped the night before upon the raw leg of an ox; and, strangely enough, it was the very night that Alexander died.

ALEXANDER.

Alexander was going on with his preparations for conquering the East. He had 12,000 foot soldiers from Macedon, trained to fight in the terrible phalanx, and 5000 horsemen; also his own bodyguard of young nobles, bred up with him at Pella; 7000 men from the Greek states, and 5000 who had been used, like the 10,000 of Xenophon, to hire themselves out to the Persians, and thus knew the languages, manners, roads, and ways of fighting in the East; but altogether he had only 34,500 men with which to attack the empire which stretched from the Ægean to Scythia, from the Euxine to the African deserts. Such was his liberality in gifts before he went away, that when he was asked what he had left for himself, he answered, "My hopes;" and his hope was not merely to conquer that great world, but to tame it, bring it into order, and teach the men there the wisdom and free spirit of the Greek world; for he had learnt from Aristotle that to make men true, brave, virtuous, and free was the way to be godlike. It was in his favour that the direct line of Persian kings had failed, and that there had been wars and factions all through the last reign. The present king was Codomanus, a grand-nephew of that Artaxerxes against whom Cyrus had led the ten thousand. He had come to the throne in 336, the same year as Alexander, and was known as Darius, the royal name he had taken. Alexander made his father's counsellor, Antipater, governor of Macedon in his absence, and took leave of his mother and his home in the spring of 334.

BACCHANALS.

## CHAP. XXVIII. — THE EXPEDITION TO PERSIA. b.c. 334.

Alexander passed the Hellespont in the April of 334, steering his own vessel, and was the first to leap on shore. The first thing he did was to go over the plain of Troy and all the scenes described in the Iliad, and then to offer sacrifices at the mound said to be the tomb of Achilles, while his chief friend Hephæstion paid the same honours to Patroclus.

The best general in the Persian army was a Rhodian named Memnon, who wanted to starve out Alexander by burning and destroying all before him; but the satrap Arsaces would not consent to this, and chose to collect his forces, and give battle to the Greeks on the banks of the river Granicus, a stream rising in Mount Ida and falling into the Euxine. Alexander led the right wing, with a white plume in his helmet, so that all might know him; Parmenio led the left; and it was a grand victory, though not without much hard fighting, hand to hand. Alexander was once in great danger, but was saved by Clitus, the son of his nurse Lanika. The Persians broke and dispersed so entirely that no army was left in Asia Minor, and the satrap Arsaces killed himself in despair.

ALEXANDER THE GREAT.

Alexander forbade his troops to plunder the country, telling them that it was his own, and that the people were as much his subjects as they were; and all the difference he made was changing the Persian governors for Greek ones. Sardis and Ephesus fell into his hands without a blow; and to assist in rebuilding the great temple of Diana, he granted all the tribute hitherto paid to the Great King. When he came to Caria, Ada, who was reigning there as queen, adopted him as her son, and wanted him to take all her best cooks with him to provide his meals for the future. He thanked her, but said his tutor had given him some far better relishers — namely, a march before daybreak as sauce for his dinner, and a light dinner as sauce for his supper.

When he came to Gordium, in Phrygia, where one version of the story of Midas had placed that king, he was shown a waggon to which the yoke was fastened by a knotted with of cornel bough, and told that in this waggon Midas had come to Gordium, and that whoever could undo it should be the lord of Asia. Alexander dextrously drew out the pin, and unwound the knot, to the delight of his followers.

In the spring he dashed down through the Taurus mountains, to take possession of the city of Tarsus, in Cilicia, before Memnon could collect the scattered Persian forces to enter it and cut him off from Syria. He rode in heated and wearied, and at once threw himself from his horse to bathe in the waters of the river Cydnus; but they came from the melting snows of the mountains, and were so exceedingly cold that the shock of the chill brought on a most dangerous fever. One physician, named Philip, offered to give him a draught that might relieve him, but at the same time a warning was sent from Parmenio that the man had been bribed to poison him. Alexander took the cup, and, while he drank it off, he held out the letter to Philip with the other hand; but happily there was no treason, and he slowly recovered, while Parmenio was sent on to secure the mountain passes. Darius, however, was advancing with a huge army, in which was a band of Spartans, who hated the Persians less than they did the Macedonians. The Persian march was a splendid sight. There was a crystal disk to represent the sun over the king's tent, and the army never moved till sunrise, when first were carried silver altars bearing the sacred fire, and followed by a band of youths, one for each day in the year, in front of the chariot of the sun, drawn by white horses; after which came a horse consecrated to the sun, and led by white-robed attendants. The king himself sat in a high, richly-adorned chariot, wearing a purple mantle, encrusted with precious stones, and encompassed with his Immortal band, in robes adorned with gold, and carrying silver-handled lances. In covered chariots were his mother Sisygambis, his chief wife and her children, and 360 inferior wives, their baggage occupying 600 mules and 300 camels, all protected by so enormous an army that everyone thought the Macedonians must be crushed.

SECOND TEMPLE OF DIANA AT EPHESUS.

With some skill, Darius' army passed from the East into Cilicia, and thus got behind Alexander, who had gone two days' march into Syria; but on the tidings he turned back at once, and found that they had not guarded the passes between him and them. So he attacked them close to Issus, and there again gained a great victory. When Darius saw his Immortals giving way, he was seized with terror, sprang out of his royal chariot, mounted on horseback, and never rested till he was on the other side of the Euphrates.

Still there was a sharp fight, and Alexander was slightly wounded in the thigh; but when all the battle was over he came to the tents of Darius, and said he would try a Persian bath. He was amused to find it a spacious curtained hall, full of vessels of gold and silver, perfumes and ointments, of which the simpler Greeks did not even know the use, and with a profusion of slaves to administer them. A Persian feast was ready also; but just as he was going to sit down to it he heard the voice of weeping and wailing in the next tent, and learned that it came from Darius' family. He rose at once to go and comfort the old mother, Sisygambis, and went into her tent with Hephæstion. Both were plainly dressed, and Hephæstion was the taller, so that the old queen took him for the king, and threw herself at his feet. When she saw her mistake she was alarmed, but Alexander consoled her gently by saying, "Be not dismayed, mother; this is Alexander's other self." And he continued to treat her with more kindness and respect than she had ever met with before, even from her own kindred; nor did he ever grieve her but once, when he showed her a robe, spun, woven, and worked by his mother and sisters for him, and offered to have her grand-children taught to make the like. Persian princesses thought it was dignified to have nothing to do, and Sisygambis fancied he meant to make slaves of them; so that he had to reassure her, and tell her that the distaff, loom, and needle were held to give honour to Greek ladies. Darius had fled beyond the rivers, and Alexander waited to follow till he should have reduced the western part of the empire. He turned into Syria and Phœnicia, and laid siege to Tyre, which was built on an island a little way from the sea-shore. He had no ships, but he began building a causeway across the water. However, the Tyrians sallied out and destroyed it; and he had to go to Sidon, which he took much more easily, and thence obtained ships, with which he beat the Tyrian fleet, and, after great toil and danger, at last entered Tyre, after a siege of five months.

Then he marched along the shore to the Philistine city of Gaza, which was likewise most bravely defended by a black slave named Bœtis. Alexander was much hurt by a stone launched from the walls, which struck him between the breast and shoulder, and when at the end of four months' siege the city was stormed, the attack was led by one of his cousins. A cruel slaughter was made of the citizens; and then Alexander marched up the steep road to Jerusalem, expecting another tedious siege. Instead of this, he beheld a long procession in white bordered with blue, coming out at the gates to meet him. All the Priests and Levites, in their robes, came forth, headed by Jaddua, the High Priest, in his beautiful raiment, and the golden mitre on his head inscribed with the words, "Holiness unto the Lord." So he had been commanded by God in a vision; and when Alexander beheld the sight, he threw himself from his horse, and adored the Name on the mitre. He told his officers that before he set out from home, when he was considering of his journey, just such a form as he now beheld had come and bidden him fear not, for he should be led into the East, and all Persia should be delivered to him. Then the High Priest took him to the outer court of the temple, and showed him the very prophecies of Daniel and Zechariah where his own conquests were foretold.

## CHAP. XXIX. ALEXANDER'S EASTERN CONQUESTS.
### b.c. 331–328.

Alexander's next step was into Egypt, where the people had long desired to drive out the Persians, and welcomed him gladly. He wished to make a Greek settlement in Egypt, and bring Greek and Egyptian learning together; so at the delta of the Nile he built the great city of Alexandria, which still remains as important as ever.

So powerful did he feel himself, that a fancy crossed his mind that, after all, he was no mere man, but the son of Jupiter, and a demigod, like Bacchus, or Hercules of old. There was a temple to the Egyptian god Ammon, on an oasis, a fertile spot round a spring in the middle of the desert, with an oracle that Alexander resolved to consult, and he made his way thither with a small chosen band. The oasis was green with laurels and palms; and the emblem of the god, a gold disk, adorned with precious stones, and placed in a huge golden ship, was carried to meet him by eighty priests, with maidens dancing round them. He was taken alone to the innermost shrine. What he heard there he never told; but after this he wore rams' horns on his helmet, because a ram's head was one sign of the god, whom the Greeks made out to be the same as Jupiter; and from this time forward he became much more proud and puffed up, so that it is likely that he had been told by this oracle just what pleased him.

He then went back to Tyre, and thence set out for the East. A bridge was thrown across the Euphrates, but the Tigris was forded by the foot soldiers, holding their shields above their heads out of the water. On the other side Darius was waiting with all the men of the East to fight for their homes, not for distant possessions, as had been the lands of Asia Minor, Syria, and Egypt. The Greeks had four days' march along the banks of the Tigris before coming in sight of the Persian host at Arbela. It was so late that the two armies slept in sight of one another. Parmenio advised the king to make a night attack, but all the answer he got was, "It would be base to steal a victory;" and when he came in the morning to say that all was ready, he found his master fast asleep, and asked him how he could rest so calmly with one of the greatest battles in the world before him. "How could we not be calm," replied Alexander, "since the enemy is coming to deliver himself into our hands?"

He would not wear such a corslet as had been crushed into his shoulder at Gaza, but put on a breastplate of thick quilted linen, girt with a broad leather belt, guarded with a crust of finely-worked metal, and holding a light, sharp sword. He had a polished steel helmet, a long spear in his right hand, and a shield on his left arm; and thus he went forth to meet Darius, who came in the midst of 200 chariots, armed with scythes, and fifteen trained elephants. He had so many troops that he intended to close the wings of his army in upon the Greeks, fold them up, and cut them off; but Alexander, foreseeing this, had warned his men to be ready to face about on any side, and then drew them up in the shape of a wedge, and thus broke into the very heart of the Immortal band, and was on the point of taking Darius prisoner, when he was called off to help Parmenio, whose division had been broken, so that the camp was threatened. Alexander's presence soon set all right again, and made the victory complete; but Darius had had time to get away, and was galloping on a swift horse to the Armenian mountains. There was nobody left to defend Assyria, and Alexander marched in through the brazen gates of Babylon, when the streets were strewn with flowers, and presents of lions and leopards borne forth to greet the conqueror.

The great temple of Bel had been partly ruined by the fire-worshipping Persians, and Alexander greatly pleased the Babylonians by decreeing that they might restore it with his aid; but the Jews at Babylon would not work at an idol temple, which they believed to be also the tower of Babel, and on their entreaty Alexander permitted them to have nothing to do with it.

After staying thirty days at Babylon, he went on to Susa, where he found the brazen statues which Xerxes had carried away from the sack of Athens. He sent them home again, to show the Greeks that he had avenged their cause. When he came to Fars — or, as the Greeks called it, Persepolis — a wretched band of Greek captives came out to meet him, with their eyes put out, or their noses, ears, hands, or feet cut off. The Greeks never tortured: it was a dreadful sight to them, and the king burst into tears, and promised to send all safe home, but they begged him, instead, to help them to live where they were, since they were ashamed to show themselves to their kindred. Their misery made Alexander decide on giving the city up to plunder; the men were killed, the women and children made slaves. He meant to revenge on the Persian capital all that the Great Kings had inflicted on the Greek cities, and one Corinthian actually shed tears of joy at seeing him on the throne, exclaiming, "What joy have those Greeks missed who have not seen Alexander on the throne of Darius!"

PRINCES OF PERSIA.

Poor Darius had pushed on into the mountains beyond Media, and thither Alexander pursued him; but his own subjects had risen against him, and placed him in a chariot bound with golden chains. Alexander dashed on in pursuit with his fleetest horsemen, riding all night, and only resting in the noonday heat, for the last twenty-five miles over a desert without water. At daybreak he saw the Persian host moving along like a confused crowd. He charged them, and there was a general flight, and presently a cry that Darius was taken. Alexander galloped up and found the unhappy king on the ground, speechless and dying, pierced with javelins by his own subjects, who would not let him fall alive into the enemy's hands, and supported by a Macedonian soldier, who had given him drink, and heard his words of gratitude to Alexander for his kindness to his family, and his hopes that the conqueror would avenge his death, and become sovereign of the world. Alexander threw his own mantle over the body, and caused it to be embalmed, and buried in the sepulchres of the Persian kings.

Now that the victory was gained, the Greeks wanted to go home, and keep all the empire subject to them; but this was not Alexander's plan. He meant to spread Greek wisdom and training over all the world, and to rule Persians as well as Greeks for their own good. So, though he let the Greek allies go home with pay, rewards, and honours, he kept his Macedonians, and called himself by the Persian title, Shah in Shah, King of Kings, crowned himself with the Persian crown, and wore royal robes on state occasions. The Macedonians could not bear the sight, especially the nobles, who had lived on almost equal terms with him. There were murmurs, and Parmenio was accused of being engaged in a plot, and put to death. It was the first sad stain on Alexander's life, and he fell into a fierce and angry mood, being fretted, as it seems, by the murmurs of the Macedonians, and harassed by the difficulties of the wild mountainous country on the borders of Persia, where he had to hunt down the last Persians who held out against him. At a town called Cyropolis, a stone thrown from the walls struck him on the back of the neck, and for some days after he could not see clearly, so that some harm had probably been done to his brain. A few days later he was foolish enough to indulge in a wine-drinking banquet, at which some flatterers began to praise him in such an absurd manner that Clitus, the son of his good foster-mother Lanika, broke out in anger at his sitting still to listen to them. "Listen to truth," he said, "or else ask no freemen to join you, but surround yourself with slaves."

Alexander, beside himself with rage, leaped up, feeling for his dagger to kill Clitus, but it was not in his belt, and they were both dragged backwards and held by their friends, until Alexander broke loose, snatched a pike from a soldier, and laid Clitus dead at his feet; but the moment he saw what he had done, he was hardly withheld from turning the point against himself, and then he shut himself up in his chamber and wept bitterly, without coming out or tasting food for three days. He caused Clitus to be buried with all honours, and offered great sacrifices to Bacchus, thinking that it was the god's hatred that made him thus pass into frenzy when he had been drinking wine.

He spent three years in securing his conquest over the Persian empire, where he won the love of the natives by his justice and kindness, and founded many cities, where he planted Greeks, and tried to make schools and patterns for the country round. They were almost all named Alexandria, and still bear the name, altered in some shape or other; but though some of his nearer friends loved him as heartily as ever, and many were proud of him, or followed him for what they could get, a great many Macedonians hated him for requiring them to set the example of respect, and laughed at the Eastern forms of state with which he was waited on, while they were still more angry that he made the Persians their equals, and not their slaves. So that he had more troubles with the Macedonians than with the strangers.

## CHAP. XXX. — THE END OF ALEXANDER. b.c. 328.

Before establishing his empire, Alexander longed to survey the unknown lands further eastwards, and he led his army down the long, terrible Khybar pass to the banks of the Indus, where he fought a great battle with an Indian king called Porus, the bravest enemy he had yet met. At last Porus was defeated and made prisoner. He came to Alexander as if he were visiting him, and Alexander received him with like courtesy, and asked if he had any request to make. "None, save to be treated as a king," said Porus. "That I shall do, for my own sake," said Alexander, and the two became friends. In this country of the Indus, Alexander received the submission of thirty-five cities, and founded two more, one of which he named Bucephala, in honour of his good horse Bucephalus, which died in the middle of a battle without a wound.

Alexander longed to press on and see all the wonders of India, and the great river Ganges, but his Macedonians were weary of the march, and absolutely refused to go any further, so that he was obliged to turn back, in hopes of collecting another army, and going to the very shores of the Eastern Ocean.

He would not, however, return by the way he had gone, through the mountains, but he built ships on the river Jhelum, a tributary of the Indus, with which to coast along the shores to the mouth of the Euphrates. There were forests of fir and pine to supply the wood, but their inhabitants, the apes and monkeys, collected in such force on the top of a hill near at hand, that the Greeks thought they were human enemies, and were about to attack them, till a native explained the mistake.

They met more dangerous enemies when they came to Mooltan, the city of a tribe called the Malli. This was a fort shut in by a strong outer wall, within which trees were growing. Alexander planted a ladder against the wall, and mounted it first, but while his men were climbing up after him, it broke, and he stood alone on the wall, a mark for all the darts of the enemy. His guards stretched up their arms, begging him to leap back to them, but he scorned to do this, and jumped down within, among the enemy. They gave back for a moment, but, on finding that he was quite alone, closed in upon him. He set his back against the wall, under a fig-tree, and slew with his sword all who approached. Then they formed into a half-circle, and shot at him with barbed arrows, six feet long. By this time a few of his guards had climbed up the wall, and were coming down to his help, at the moment when an arrow pierced his breast, and he sank down in a kneeling posture, with his brow on the rim of his shield, while his men held their shields over him till the rest could come to their aid, and he was taken up as one dead, and carried out on his shield, while all within the fort were slaughtered in the rage of the Macedonians. When the king had been carried to his tent, the point of the arrow was found to be firmly fixed in his breast-bone, and he bade Perdiccas, his friend, cut a gash wide enough to allow the barbs to pass before drawing it out. He refused to be held while this was done, but kept himself perfectly still, until he fainted, and lay for many hours between life and death; nor was it for a week that he could even bear to be placed on board a galley, and lie on the deck under an awning as it went down the river, whilst his men were in raptures to see him restored to them.

He had to halt for some weeks, and then proceed along the Indus, until he reached the Indian Ocean, where the Greeks were delighted to see their old friend the sea, though they were amazed at the tides, having never seen any in their own Mediterranean. Alexander now sent an old commander, Nearchus, to take charge of the ships along the coast, while he himself marched along inland, to collect provisions and dig wells for their supply; but the dreadful, bare, waterless country, covered with rocks, is so unfit for men that his troops suffered exceedingly, and hardly anyone has been there since his time. He shared all the distresses of his soldiers, and once, when a little water, found with great difficulty, was brought him as he plodded along in the scorching heat of a noonday sun, he gave heartfelt thanks, but in the sight of all poured out the water, not choosing to take to himself what all could not share. In the midst the guides lost their way, and Alexander had to steer their course for a week by his own instinct, and the sun and stars, until after sixty days he reached a place which seems to be Bunpore, part of the Persian empire, where his difficulties were over, and Nearchus by-and-by joined him, after a wonderful voyage, of which he wrote an account, which has not come down to our times, so that we only know that no Greek believed in it. Alexander meant to try if he could sail through this strange sea, and return to Greece by the Pillars of Hercules, as we now know would have been quite possible.

He found, when he came back to Persia, that the governors he had left in the cities had thought that he was sure to perish in India, and had plundered shamefully, so that he had to punish severely both Greeks and Persians; but then, to make the two nations friends, he held an immense wedding feast at Susa, when eighty Greek bridegrooms married eighty Persian brides. Alexander himself and his friend Hephæstion had the two daughters of Darius, and the other ladies were daughters of satraps. The wedding was thus conducted: in one great hall eighty double seats were placed, and here the bridegrooms sat down to feast, till the brides entered, in jewelled turbans, wide linen drawers, silken tunics, and broad belts. Alexander rose, took his princess by the hand, and led her to his seat, and all the rest followed his example — each led his lady to his seat, kissed her, and placed her beside him, then cut a loaf of bread in two, poured out wine, and ate and drank with her.

SUPPOSED WALLS OF BABYLON—From an ancient coin.

Hephæstion died soon after, at Ecbatana, of a fever he had not taken care of in time. Alexander caused his corpse to be brought to Babylon, and burnt on a funeral pile; while he himself was in an agony of grief, and sent to ask the oracle of Ammon whether his friend might not be worshipped as a hero-god. He himself had already demanded divine honours from the Greeks. The Athenians obeyed, but secretly mocked; and the Spartans grimly answered, "If Alexander will be a god, let him."

Alexander was at Babylon, newly fortifying it, and preparing it to be the capital of his mighty empire. He held his court seated on the golden throne of the Persian Shahs, with a golden pine over it, the leaves of emeralds and the fruit of carbuncles; and here he received embassies from every known people in Europe and Asia, and stood at the highest point of glory that man has ever reached, not knowing how near the end was.

Ever since Cyrus had taken Babylon by turning the Euphrates out of its course, the ground had been ill drained, swampy, and unhealthy; and before setting out on further conquests, Alexander wished to put all this in order again, and went about in a boat on the canals to give directions. His broad-brimmed hat was blown off, and lodged among the weeping willows round some old Assyrian's tomb; and though it was brought back at once, the Greeks thought its having been on a tomb an evil omen, but the real harm was in the heat of the sun on his bare head, which he had shorn in mourning for Hephæstion.

He meant to go on an expedition to Arabia, and offered a great sacrifice, but at night fever came on. The Greeks at home, who hated him, said it was from drinking a huge cup of wine at one draught; but this is almost certain not to be true, since his doctors have left a daily journal of his illness, and make no mention of any such excess. He daily grew worse, worn out by his toils and his wounds, and soon he sank into a lethargy, in which he hardly spoke. Once he said something about his empire passing to the strongest, and of great strife at his funeral games, and at last, when his breath was almost gone, he held out his signet ring to Perdiccas, the only one of his old friends who was near him. He was only thirty-three years old, and had made his mighty conquests in twelve years, when he thus died in 323. The poor old Persian queen, Sisygambis, so grieved for him that she refused all food, sat weeping in a corner, and died a few days after him.

### CHAP. XXXI. THE LAST STRUGGLES OF ATHENS. b.c. 334–311.

The generals of Alexander met in dismay and grief the morning after his death at Babylon, and Perdiccas sadly laid the ring on the empty throne. There was no one to go on with what he had begun, for though he had a brother named Arridæus, the poor youth was weak in mind; and Alexander's own son was a little, helpless infant. These two were joined together as Kings of Macedon and Shahs of Persia, and four guardians were appointed for them, who really only used their names as a means of getting power for themselves.

The Greek cities had always hated the yoke of Macedon, and hoped that Alexander would be lost in the East. They had been restless all this time, and had only been kept down by the threats and the bribes of Antipater, the governor of Macedon. When the news of Alexander's death first came to Athens, the people were ready to make a great outbreak, but the more cautious would not believe it, and Phocion advised them to wait, "for," he said, "if he is dead to-day, he will still be dead to-morrow and the next day, so that we may take council at our leisure."

Phocion was a good and honest man, but low-spirited, and he thought quiet the only hope for Athens. When he found that the citizens were making a great boasting, and were ready to rush into a war without counting the cost, he said he would advise one only "whenever he saw the young men ready to keep their ranks, the old men to pay the money, and the orators to abstain from taking it for themselves." However, the Athenians made a league with the Thessalians and other Greeks against Macedon, and put their army under the command of Leosthenes, a young man to whom Phocion said, "Your speeches are like cypress trees, stately and lofty, but bearing no fruit."

Leosthenes defeated Antipater and the Macedonians at Lamia, and besieged them; but still Phocion had no hope, and when asked whether he could wish for better success, he said, "No, but better counsels."

Demosthenes had in the meantime been banished by the spite of some of his secret enemies. He was very angry and bitter, and as he lived in Ægina, whence he could still see the Acropolis and temple of Pallas Athene, he exclaimed, "Goddess, what favourites thou halt chosen — the owl, the ass, and the Athenians;" but in these days of joy a ship was sent by the State to bring him home, and fifty talents were granted to him.

But Leosthenes was killed by a stone from the walls of Lamia, and some Macedonian troops came home from the East to the help of Antipater. They were defeated by land, but they beat the Athenians by sea; and in a second battle such a defeat was given to the Greeks that their league against Macedon was broken up, and each city was obliged to make peace for itself separately.

GATE OF HADRIAN IN ATHENS.

Antipater made it a condition of granting peace that all who had favoured resistance to Macedon should be treated as rebels. Demosthenes and his friends fled from Athens, and took refuge at the temples of different gods; but the cruel Macedonian was resolved that they should all be put to death, and took a set of ruffians into his pay, who were called the Exile-hunters, because they were to search out and kill all who had been sent away from their cities for urging them to free themselves. Demosthenes was in the temple of Neptune at Calaurea. When the exile-hunters came thither, he desired time to write a letter to his friends, spread a roll of parchment before him, and bit the top of the reed he was writing with; after which he bowed his head, and covered it with his robe. There was poison hidden in the top of the reed, and presently he rose up and said, "Act the part of Creon, and throw my body to the dogs. I quit thy sanctuary, Neptune, still breathing, though Antipater and the Macedonians have not spared it from pollution."

He tried to reach the door, but as he passed the altar, fell, and died with one groan. Poor Athens was quite struck down, and the affairs were chiefly managed by Phocion, who was a thoroughly honest, upright man, but submitted to let the Macedonians dictate to the city, because he did not think the Athenians could make head against them. Antipater could never persuade him to take any reward for himself, though others who were friends of Macedon could never be satisfied with bribes. Meantime, Perdiccas was coming home, bringing with him the two young kings, uncle and nephew, and meaning to put Antipater down; but he turned aside on his way to attack Ptolemy, the ablest of all Alexander's generals, who was commanding in Egypt, and in trying to cross the Nile a great part of his army was cut off, and multitudes were eaten by the crocodiles. The few who were left rose against him and murdered him in his tent, then offered the command and guardianship of the kings to Ptolemy; but he would not take it, and chose rather to stay and make himself king of Egypt, where his family reigned at Alexandria for three hundred years, all the kings being called Ptolemy.

Antipater was by this time an old man, and he died a little after; and his son Cassander expected to take the government of Macedon, but, to his surprise, found that his father had appointed the old general Polysperchon in his stead. This he would not endure, and a war arose between the two. One of Cassander's friends took possession of the Piræus, to hold it for him; and Phocion was accused of having advised it, and was obliged to flee with his friends into a village in Phocis, where they were made prisoners by Polysperchon, who thought to please the Athenians by sending them in waggons to Athens to be tried. A mob of the worst sort came together, and would not hear their defence, but sentenced them to die by taking hemlock. When Phocion was asked whether he had any message for his son, he said, "Only that he bear no grudge against the Athenians." There was not enough hemlock to poison all, and more was sent for. The jailer desired to be paid, and Phocion said, "Give the man his money. One cannot even die for nothing in Athens."

Phocion is sometimes called the last of the Athenians, but it was a sad kind of greatness, for he could not give them freedom, and only tried to keep them from the misery of war by submission to Macedon. The Spartans would give no help; and though the little city of Megalopolis held bravely out against Cassander, it was taken and horribly punished; and it was plain that the old spirit of the Greeks was gone, and that they could no longer band together to keep out the enemy; so they all remained in subjection to Macedon, most of them with a garrison of Macedonian soldiers in their citadel. But Athens was as full of philosophers as ever, and became a sort of college, where people sent their sons to study learning, oratory, and poetry, and hear the disputes of the Stoic and Epicurean philosophers.

In the meantime Alexander's embalmed body had been buried at Alexandria, and the two young kings, his son Alexander Ægos and his half-brother Arridæus, had been brought to Macedon. His mother Olympias put poor Arridæus to death as soon as she could get him into her power. She had always hated Antipater, and now took part with Polysperchon against Cassander; but this was the losing side. Polysperchon was beaten, and driven out of Macedon: and she, with her grandson and his mother, the Persian princess Roxana, shut themselves up in Pydna, where Cassander besieged them till he had starved them out, and Olympias surrendered on condition that her life was spared; but Cassander did not keep his word, and sent soldiers to put her to death. The young king and his mother were kept at Amphipolis till the boy was sixteen years old; and then, growing afraid that he would try to win his father's throne, Cassander had them both slain.

So the great empire of Alexander was broken up among four chief powers, Cassander in Macedon, Lysimachus in Thrace, Seleucus in Syria, Ptolemy in Egypt.

## CHAP. XXXII. — THE FOUR NEW KINGDOMS. b.c. 311-287.

There was a mighty power coming up against Cassander. One of Alexander's old generals, named Antigonus, the "One-eyed," had received some Asiatic provinces for his share in the break-up of the empire, and when Perdiccas set out on his return was appointed commander in his stead in the East; and again, when Antipater died, Polysperchon renewed his appointment; while Eumenes, an honest and good man, was the regent upheld by Cassander's party. In 316 a battle was fought at Gabiene, in which Eumenes was defeated. He was given up to Antigonus by his own troops, and as the victor could not bear to kill his old comrade, he left him in prison to be starved to death.

Then Antigonus took possession of all the treasures in Ecbatana and Babylon, and began to call Seleucus in Syria to account for his dealings with the revenues of the empire. Seleucus fled into Egypt; and all the four chiefs, Ptolemy, Seleucus, Lysimachus, and Cassander joined together to put down Antigonus and his brave and able son, Demetrius. There was war everywhere, until in 311 peace was made, on condition that the Greek cities should be set free, and that Antigonus should have the whole government of Asia Minor, Seleucus of Syria, Ptolemy of Egypt, Cassander of Macedon, and Lysimachus of Thrace, till the young Alexander was old enough to govern; but, as we have seen, Cassander murdered him when he was only sixteen, and the old family of Macedon was at an end. Nor did Cassander give up the Greek cities; so Demetrius was sent to force him to do so. There was little attempt to resist him; and the Athenians were in such delight that they called him the Saviour, named a month after him, lodged him in the Parthenon itself, and caused his image to be carried in processions among those of the gods themselves. He took so many towns that his name in history is Poliorketes, or the City-taker, and then he was sent to gain the isle of Cyprus from Ptolemy. The fleet of Alexandria was thought the best in the world, but Demetrius defeated it entirely in the year 306, and in their joy the soldiers called him and his father both kings, and they put on the diadem of the Shahs of Persia, making their capital the city they had founded on the Orontes, and calling it Antigoneia.

Cassander, Ptolemy, Lysimachus, and Seleucus all likewise called themselves kings. And still the war went on. Demetrius was sent against the island of Rhodes, which belonged to Ptolemy, and besieged the city a whole year, but could not take it, and was obliged to make peace with the islanders at last, and to give them all the machines he had used in the siege. These they sold for 300 talents, and used the money to make an enormous brazen statue of Apollo, to stand with one foot on each side of the entrance of the harbour. Ships in full sail could pass under it, and few men could grasp its thumb with their arms. It was called the Colossus of Rhodes, and was counted as the seventh wonder of the world, the others being the Temple of Diana at Ephesus, the Tomb of Mausolus, the Lighthouse of Messina, the Walls of Babylon, the Labyrinth of Crete, and the Pyramids of Egypt. They also consecrated a grove to Ptolemy for the assistance he had given to them.

Demetrius then went to Greece, and tried to overthrow Cassander, but the other kings joined against him, and he was obliged to go home, for Seleucus was threatening Antigoneia. Antigonus and Demetrius collected their forces, and fought a great battle at Ipsus, where Seleucus brought trained elephants from India, which had lately begun to be used in battle, and were found to frighten horses so as to render them quite unmanageable. Demetrius, however, thought he had gained the victory, but he rushed on too fast, and left his father unsupported, so that poor old Antigonus, who was eighty years of age, was shut in by the troops of Seleucus and killed. Demetrius had to retreat to Ephesus with his broken army.

The Athenians, who had made so much of him before, now turned against him, and made a law to punish with death anyone who should speak of making peace with him. However, Cassander died, and his sons quarrelled about the kingdom, so that Demetrius found it a good opportunity to return to Greece, and very soon made the Athenians open their gates to him, which they did in fear and trembling; but he treated them so mercifully that they soon admired him as much as ever.

MACEDONIAN SOLDIER.

Then he attacked Sparta, and defeated her king, taking the city which had so long held out against the Macedonians; but he had only just done so when he heard that Ptolemy had recovered all Cyprus except Salamina, and that Lysimachus had seized all Asia Minor, so that nothing was left to him but his army.

But there was a wonderful change still to befall him. Cassander's sons, — as has been said, were disputing for the kingdom. Their mother, Thessalonica, a daughter of Philip of Macedon, favoured the youngest, and this so enraged the eldest that he killed her with his own hand. His brother called on Demetrius to help him, and he came with his army; but on some fancy that the youth was plotting against him, he had him put to death, and convinced the Macedonians that the act was just. They would not have the murderer of his own mother as their king, but chose Demetrius himself to be king of Macedon, so that almost at the same time he lost one kingdom and gained another, and this last remained in his family for several generations. He tried to regain Asia, but did not succeed; indeed he was once again obliged to fly from Macedonia in disguise. He had learned to admire the splendours of the East, wore a double diadem on his head, and wonderful sandals; and he had also ordered skilful weavers and embroiderers to make him a mantle, on which the system of the universe as then understood — the earth in the centre, with the moon, sun, and planets, and every fixed star then discovered — was to be embroidered in gold.

The Macedonians had not been used to see their kings crowned at all, or differently dressed from themselves, and they had hardly borne such assumption of state from Alexander himself, in the height of his pomp and glory, and when he had newly taken the throne of the kings of Persia; and they were much offended at Demetrius' splendour, and still more at his pride and haughtiness of manner, and inattention to those who had to make any request from him.

One day, when he was passing through the streets, some persons brought him some petitions, which he received more graciously than usual, and placed them in one of the folds of his robe; but as soon as he came to a bridge over a river he threw them into the water, to the great offence and disappointment of the poor people who had brought them.

This was very unlike Ptolemy, who was a wise, clear-headed man, with much of Alexander's spirit of teaching and improving people under him, and who ruled so as to make himself much beloved in Egypt, Cyprus, Rhodes, and Palestine. The new city of Alexandria was his capital, and under him and his son Ptolemy Philadelphus it grew to be a great merchant city, and also a school of art, science, and philosophy almost as famous as Athens, and with a library containing all the chief books in the world, including the Old Testament. This was translated into Greek by 70 learned Jews, and therefore called the Septuagint.

Seleucus, king of Syria, held all the lands from Persia to Asia Minor. His capital was Antioch, in Syria, which he had built and named after his son Antiochus, and which became a very splendid and beautiful city, full of a light-minded, merry people, fond of games and shows. He built many other places, calling them after himself or his son, and placing Greeks to live in them. Thus, though Alexander only reigned twelve years, he had made a great difference to the world, for the Greek language, learning, and habits were spread all over the East, and every well-taught person was brought up in them. So that, while the grand old Greek states were in bondage, and produced no more great men, their teachings had spread farther than they ever thought.

## CHAP. XXXIII — PYRRHUS, KING OF EPIRUS. b.c. 287.

To the westward of Greece lay a mountainous land, bordered by the Adriatic Sea, and in old times called Epirus. The people spoke a sort of barbarous Greek, worse than that of the Macedonians; but the royal family were pure Greeks, and believed themselves to be descended from Achilles; and Alexander's mother, Olympias, had been one of them. In the wars and confusion that followed upon Alexander's death, the Epirot king, Æacides, took part, and this led to a rising against him, ending in his being killed, with all his family, except his little two-year-old son, named Pyrrhus, who was saved by some faithful servants. They fled towards the city of Megara, on the border of Macedon, but they only reached it late at night, and there was a rough and rapid river between, swelled by rains. They called to the people on the other side, and held up the little child, but the rushing of the river drowned their voices, and their words were not understood. At last one of them peeled off a piece of bark from an oak tree, and scratched on it with the tongue of a buckle an account of their distress, and, fastening it to a stone, threw it over. The Megarians immediately made a sort of raft with trees, and, floating over, brought little Pyrrhus and his friends across; but finding Macedon not safe, since Cassander had been the enemy of Æacides, they went on to Illyria, where they found the king, Glaucias, sitting with his queen. Putting the child on the ground, they began to tell their story. At first the king was unwilling to grant him shelter, being afraid of Cassander; but the little fellow, crawling about, presently came near, and, laying hold of his leg, pulled himself upon his feet, and looked up in his face. The pretty, unconscious action of a suppliant so moved Glaucias that he took him up in his arms, and gave him into those of the queen, bidding her have him bred up among their own children;

and though Cassander offered 200 talents, he would not give up the boy.

When Pyrrhus was twelve years old, Glaucias sent an army to restore him to his throne, and guarded him there. He was high-spirited, brave, and gracious, but remarkable-looking, from his upper teeth being all in one, without divisions. When he was seventeen, while he was gone to Illyria to the wedding of one of Glaucias' sons, his subjects rose against him, and made one of his cousins king. He then went to Demetrius, who had married his elder sister, and fought under him at the battle of Ipsus; after which Demetrius sent him as a hostage to Alexandria, and his grace and spirit made him so great a favourite with Ptolemy that he gave him his step-daughter Berenice in marriage, and helped him to raise an army with which he recovered his kingdom of Epirus.

He had not long been settled there before the Macedonians, who had begun to hate Demetrius, heard such accounts of Pyrrhus' kindness as a man and skill as a warrior, that the next time a war broke out they all deserted Demetrius, who was forced to fly in the disguise of a common soldier, and his wife poisoned herself in despair. However, Demetrius did not lose courage, but left his son Antigonus to protect Greece, and went into Asia Minor, hoping to win back some of his father's old kingdom from Seleucus, but he could get nobody to join him; and after wandering about in hunger and distress in the Cilician mountains, he was forced to give himself up a prisoner to Seleucus, who kept him in captivity, but treated him kindly, and let him hunt in the royal park. His son Antigonus, however, who still held Greece, wrote to offer himself as a hostage, that his father might be set free; but before he could reach Syria, Demetrius the City-taker had died of over-eating and drinking in his captivity, and only the urn containing his ashes could be sent to his son in Greece.

Pyrrhus had not kept Macedon long, for Lysimachus attacked him, and the fickle Macedonians all went over to the Thracian, so that he was obliged to retreat into his own kingdom of Epirus; whilst Seleucus and Lysimachus began a war, in which Lysimachus was killed; and thus both Thrace and Macedon were in the hands of Seleucus, who is therefore commonly called the Conqueror. He was the last survivor of all Alexander's generals, and held all his empire except Egypt; but while taking possession of Macedonia he was murdered by a vile Egyptian Greek, whom he had befriended, named Ptolemy Keraunus. This man, in the confusion that followed, managed to make himself king of Macedon.

But just at this time the Kelts, or Gauls, the same race who used to dwell in Britain and Gaul, made one of their great inroads from the mountains. The Macedonians thought them mere savages, easy to conquer; but it turned out quite otherwise. The Kelts defeated them entirely, cut off Ptolemy Keraunus' head, and carried it about upon a pole, and overran all Thrace and Macedon. Then they advanced to the Pass of Thermopylæ, found the way over Mount Œta by which Xerxes had surprised the Spartans, and were about to plunder Delphi, their Bran, or chief, being reported to say that the gods did not want riches as much as men did. The Greeks, in much grief for their beloved sanctuary, assembled to fight for it, and they were aided by a terrible storm and earthquake, which dismayed the Gauls, so that the next morning they were in a dispirited state, and could not stand against the Greeks. The Bran was wounded, and finding that the battle was lost, called the other chiefs round him, advised them to kill all the wounded men, and make their retreat as best they might, and then stabbed himself to set the example. The others tried to retreat, but were set upon by the Greeks, tormented, and starved; and it is said that all who had marched to Delphi perished, and the only Gauls of all this host who survived were a party who had crossed the Hellespont, and made a settlement in the very heart of Asia Minor, where they were known by the name of Galatians, and still kept up their own language.

DELPHI AND THE CASTALIAN FOUNT.

When they had thus cut off Keraunus, Antigonus came from Greece, and took possession of Macedon. He made a treaty with Antiochus, who had succeeded his father Seleucus in Syria, and thenceforth the family founded by Antigonus the One-eyed held Macedon. This Antigonus is called Gonatas, from the name of a guard for the knee which he wore.

Pyrrhus, in the meantime, set out on a wild expedition to help the Greek colonies in Italy against the Romans, hoping to make himself as famous in the West as Alexander had done in the East; but the story of his doings there belongs to the history of Rome, so that I will leave it. He was absent six years, and came home unsuccessful to harass Antigonus again. For a few years the Macedonians again went over to Pyrrhus, and he tried to conquer Greece, marching against Sparta with 25,000 men, 2000 horse, and 24 elephants. He assaulted the city, but Spartan bravery was still enough to beat him off twice. However, he wintered in the Peloponnesus, and in the spring attacked the city of Argos, which was watched over by Antigonus, with his army, on a hill near at hand. Pyrrhus had shown himself so skilful a general that

Antigonus would not fight a battle with him, and at night some traitors invited Pyrrhus into Argos, with some of his troops; but another party admitted Antigonus' son and his forces. In the morning Pyrrhus saw how he had been caught, and sent a message to his son Helenus outside to break down part of the wall, that he might retreat; but there was some blunder in the message, and Helenus thought he was to come in to help his father, so his men going in and Pyrrhus' going out met in the gateway and choked it. Matters were made worse by one of the elephants falling down and blocking up the street, while another went mad, and ran about trampling down the crowd and trumpeting. Pyrrhus kept in the rear, trying to guard his men through the streets, when an Argive slightly wounded him, and as he was rushing to revenge the blow, the mother of the man, who was looking down from her window above, threw down a tile, hoping to save him, and struck Pyrrhus on the back of the neck. He fell down stunned, and a soldier cut off his head, and carried it to Antigonus, who turned away in tears at the sight of this sad remnant of the ablest captain in Greece, and caused Pyrrhus' body to be honourably buried in the temple of Ceres. Pyrrhus was only forty-six years old when he was thus slain in the year 272.

There is a story of a conversation between Pyrrhus and a philosopher named Kineas, just as he was setting off for Italy. "What shall you do with these men?" asked Kineas. "Overcome Italy and Rome," said Pyrrhus. "And what next?" "Then Sicily will be easily conquered." "Is that all?" "Oh no; Carthage and Lybia may be subdued next." "And then?" "Then we may secure Macedon and Greece." "And then?" "Then we may eat and drink and discourse." "And pray," said Kineas, "why should we not do so at once?"

## CHAP. XXXIV. ARATUS AND THE ACHAIAN LEAGUE. b.c. 267.

Antigonus Gonatas was now quite the most powerful person left in Macedon or Greece, and though Sparta and Athens tried to get the help of Egypt against him, they could do nothing to shake off his power.

There were twelve little cities in the Peloponnesus, which were all united together in one league, called the Achaian, each governing itself, but all joining together against any enemy outside. In the good old times they had sent men to the wars as allies of Sparta, but they had never had a man of much mark among them. In the evil times, Sicyon, a city near Achaia, fell under the power of a tyrant, and about the time that Pyrrhus was killed, Clinias, a citizen of Sicyon, made a great attempt to free his townsmen, but he was found out, his house attacked, and he and his family all put to death, except his son Aratus, a little boy of seven years old, who ran away from the dreadful sight, and went wandering about the town, till by chance he came into the house of the tyrant's sister. She took pity on the poor boy, hid him from her brother all day, and at night sent him to Argos to some friends of his father, by whom he was brought up.

When he was only twenty he wrote to friends at Sicyon, and finding them of the same mind with himself, he climbed the walls at night and met them. The people gathered round him, and he caused it to be proclaimed with a loud voice, "Aratus, the son of Clinias, calls on Sicyon to resume her liberty." The people all began rushing to the tyrant's house. He fled by an underground passage, and his house was set on fire, but not one person on either side was killed or wounded. Aratus was resolved to keep Sicyon free, and in order to make her strong enough, he persuaded the citizens to join her to the Achaian League; and he soon became the leading man among all the

Achaians, and his example made other cities come into the same band of union. He further tried to gain strength by an alliance with Egypt, and he went thither to see Ptolemy III., called Euergetes, or the Benefactor. It is said that Ptolemy's good-will was won by Aratus' love of art, and especially of pictures. Apelles, the greatest Grecian painter, was then living, and had taken a portrait of one of the tyrants of Sicyon. Aratus had destroyed all their likenesses, and he stood a long time looking at this one before he could bring himself to condemn it, but at last he made up his mind that it must not be spared. Ptolemy liked him so much that he granted him 150 talents for the city, and the Achaians were so much pleased that they twice elected him their general, and the second time he did them a great service.

CORINTH.

In the middle of the Isthmus of Corinth stood the city, and in the midst was a fort called Acro-Corinthus, perched on a high hill in the very centre of the city, so that whoever held it was master of all to the south, and old Philip of Macedon used to call it the Corinthian shackles of Greece. The king of Macedon, Antigonus III., now held it; but Aratus devised a scheme to take it. A Corinthian named Erginus had come to Sicyon on business, and there met a friend of Aratus, to whom he chanced to mention that there was a narrow path leading up to the Acro-Corinthus at a place where the wall was low. Aratus heard of this, and promised Erginus sixty talents if he would guide him to the spot; but as he had not the money, he placed all his gold and silver plate and his wife's jewels in pledge for the amount.

On the appointed night Aratus came with 400 men, carrying scaling-ladders, and placed them in the temple of Juno, outside the city, where they all sat down and took off their shoes. A heavy fog came on, and entirely hid them; and Aratus, with 100 picked men, came to the rock at the foot of the city wall, and there waited while Erginus and seven others, dressed as travellers, went to the gates and killed the sentinel and guard, without an alarm. Then the ladders were fixed, and Aratus came up with his men, and stood under the wall unseen, while four men with lights passed by them. Three of these they killed, but the fourth escaped, and gave the alarm. The trumpets were sounded, and every street was full of lights and swarmed with men; but Aratus, meantime, was trying to climb the steep rocks, and groping for the path leading up to the citadel. Happily the fog lifted for a moment, the moon shone out, and he saw his way, and hastened up to the Acro-Corinthus, where he began to fight with the astonished garrison. The 300 men whom he had left in the temple of Juno heard the noise in the city and saw the lights, then marched in and came to the foot of the rock, but not being able to find the path, they drew up at the foot of a precipice, sheltered by an overhanging rock, and there waited in much anxiety, hearing the battle overhead, but not able to join in it. The Macedonian governor, in the meantime, had called out his men, and was going up to support the guard in the fort, blowing his trumpets, when, as he passed these men, they dashed out on him, just as if they had been put in ambush on purpose, and so dismayed them in the confusion that they fancied the enemy five times as many, as the moon and the torches flashed on their armour, and they let themselves all be made prisoners.

VIEW LOOKING ACROSS ISTHMUS OF CORINTH.

By the time morning had come Corinth was in the hands of the Achaians, and Aratus came down from the fortress to meet the people in the theatre. His 400 men were drawn up in two lines at its entrances, and the Corinthians filled the seats, and shouted with an ecstasy of joy, for it was the first time for nearly a century that true Greeks had gained any advantage over Macedonians. Aratus was worn out by anxiety, his long march, and night of fighting, and as he stood leaning on his spear he could hardly rally strength to address them, and while giving back to them the keys of their city, which they had never had since Philip's time, he exhorted them to join the League, which they did. The Macedonians were expelled, and Aratus put an Achaian garrison into the Acro-Corinthus.

His whole care was to get Greece free from the Macedonians, and he drove them out from city after city, persuading each to join the Achaian League as it was delivered. Argos was still under a tyrant named Aristippus, and Aratus made many attempts to turn him out, by his usual fashion of night attacks. Once he got into the city, and fought there all day, though he was wounded with a lance in the thigh; but he was obliged to retreat at night. However, he attacked the tyrant when out on an expedition, and slew him, but still could not set Argos free, as the tyrant's son Aristomenes still held it.

However, Lysiades, the tyrant of Megalopolis, was so moved by admiration for the patriot that he resigned, and the city joined the League. In fact, Aratus was at this time quite the greatest man in Greece. He beat the Ætolians, when they were on a foray into the Achaian territories, and forced them to make peace; and he tried also to win Athens and Sparta to the common cause against Macedon, but there were jealousies in the way that hindered his success, and all his enterprises were rendered more difficult by his weakly health, which always made him suffer greatly from the fatigue and excitement of a battle.

RUINS OF A TEMPLE AT CORINTH.

## CHAP. XXXV. AGIS AND THE REVIVAL OF SPARTA.
### b.c. 244–236.

Sparta had never been so overcome by Macedon as the states north of the Isthmus, but all the discipline of Lycurgus had been forgotten, and the Ephors and Kings had become greedy, idle, and corrupt. One of the kings, named Leonidas, had gone to Antioch, married an Eastern wife, and learned all the Syrian and Persian vanities in which King Seleucus delighted, and he brought these home to Sparta. The other king, Eudamidas, was such a miser, that on his death, in 244, his widow and his mother were said to possess more gold than all the rest of the people in the state put together; but he left a son of nineteen, named Agis, most unlike himself.

As soon as, in his childhood, Agis had heard the story of his great forefathers, he set himself to live like an ancient Spartan, giving up whatever Lycurgus had forbidden, dressing and eating as plainly as he could, and always saying that he would not be king if he did not hope to make Sparta her true self again. When he became king, he was seen in the usual dress of a Greek, uncrowned, as the first Leonidas and Agesilaus had been; while the other king, ill named Leonidas, moved about in a diadem and purple robes and jewels, like a Persian Shah.

Agis was resolved to bring back all the old rule. There were but 700 old Dorian Spartans left, and only about 100 of these still had their family estates, while the others were starving; and most of the property was in the hands of women. Therefore the young king was resolved to have all given up and divided again, and he prevailed on his mother and grandmother to throw all their wealth into the common stock, as also his mother's brother Agesilaus, who was willing, because he was so much in debt that he could hardly lose by any change. The other ladies made a great outcry, and Leonidas was very angry, but he did not dare to hinder all this, because all the high-born men, who had been so poor, were on the young king's side.

So there was a public assembly, and one of the Ephors proposed the reform, showing how ease and pleasure had brought their city low, and how hardihood and courage might yet bring back her true greatness. Leonidas spoke against the changes, but Agis argued with such fire and force that he won over all that were high-minded enough to understand him, and in especial Cleombrotus, the son-in-law of Leonidas. Agis laid down before the assembly all his father's vast hoards, and his example was followed by many; but the other king put such difficulties in the way that the reformers found that they could do nothing unless they removed him, so they brought forward an old law, which forbade that any son of Hercules should reign who had married a foreign woman, or sojourned in a strange land.

On hearing of this, Leonidas took refuge in the temple of Athene, and as he did not appear when he was summoned before the Ephors, they deposed him, and named Cleombrotus in his stead; but when Agis found there was a plan for killing the old king, he took care to send him away in safety to Tegea, with his daughter Chilonis, who clave to him in trouble.

Agis thought his uncle Agesilaus was heartily with the change, and so had him chosen one of the Ephors; but, in truth, all Agesilaus wanted was to be free from his debts, and he persuaded the young king that the lands could not be freshly divided till all debts had been cancelled. So all the bonds were brought into the market-place and burnt, while Agesilaus cried out that he had never seen so fine a fire; but having done this, he was resolved not to part with his wealth, and delayed till the Ætolians made an attack on the Peloponnesus, and Aratus called on Sparta to assist the Achaians. Agis was sent at the head of an army to the Isthmus, and there behaved like an ancient Spartan king, sharing all the toils and hardships of the soldiers, and wearing nothing to distinguish him from them; but while he was away everything had gone wrong at Sparta; people had gone back to their old bad habits, and Agesilaus was using his office of Ephor so shamefully that he had been obliged to have a guard of soldiers to protect him from the people. This behaviour had made the people suspect his nephew of being dishonest in his reforms, and they had sent to recall Leonidas.

Agesilaus fled, and Agis was obliged to take sanctuary in Athene's temple, and Cleombrotus in that of Neptune, where Leonidas found him. His wife Chilonis, with her two little children, threw herself between him and her father, pleading for his life, and promising he should leave the city; and Leonidas listened, trying to make her remain, but she clung to her husband, and went into exile with him.

Agiatis, the young wife of Agis, could not join him in the temple, being kept at home by the birth of her first babe. He never left the sanctuary, except to go to the baths, to which he was guarded by armed friends. At last two of these were bribed to betray him. One said, "Agis, I must take you to the Ephors," and the other threw a cloak over his head; while Leonidas came up with a guard of foreign soldiers and dragged him to prison, where the Ephors came to examine him. One asked him if he repented. "I can never repent of virtue," he said.

They sentenced him to die; and finding that his mother and grandmother were trying to stir up the people to demand that he should be heard in public, they sent the executioners at once to put him to death. One of them came in tears, but Agis quickly said, "Weep not, friend; I am happier than those who condemn me;" and he held out his neck for the rope which strangled him just as his grandmother and mother came in. The grandmother was strangled the next moment. The mother said, "May this be for the good of Sparta," and after laying out the limbs of her son and mother, was also put to death; and the young widow Agiatis, with her babe, was carried to the house of Leonidas. The reform of Agis had lasted only three years, and he was but twenty-two, when his plans were thus cruelly cut short.

Leonidas was thus left to reign alone, the first time such a thing had happened in Sparta. As poor Agiatis was a rich heiress, he kept her in his house, and married her to his son Cleomenes, a mere boy, much younger than herself. She was the fairest and wisest woman in Greece; and though she always was cold, grave, and stern towards the wicked old king, she loved his wife, and was gentle towards the young boy, who was blameless of his father's sin, and gave her all his heart for his whole life. He cared for nothing so much as to hear from her of Agis, his brave, self-denying ways, and noble plans; and thus did they live, after the untimely death of Agis, strengthened by the study of the Stoic philosophy, which taught that virtue was the highest good, and that no suffering, not even death, was to be shunned in pursuit of her.

When Leonidas died, in 236, Cleomenes became the only king, but he was so young that Aratus and the Achaians thought it a good time for extending the power of their league at the expense of Sparta; so, though no war was going on, Aratus sent a troop by night to seize Tegea and Orchomenus, cities in alliance with Sparta. But his designs were found out in time for Cleomenes to strengthen the garrisons in both places, and march himself to a place called the Athenæum, which guarded one of the passes into Laconia.

This made the attempt fail, and Cleomenes wrote to ask the cause of the night march of the Achaians. Aratus answered that it was to hinder the fortification of the Athenæum.

"What was the use, then, of torches and scaling-ladders?" asked Cleomenes.

Aratus laughed, and asked a Spartan who was in exile what kind of youth this young king was; and the Spartan made reply, "If you have any designs against Sparta, you had better begin them before the game chicken's spurs are grown."

It was a great pity that these two free states in Laconia and Achaia were only wasting their strength against each other, instead of joining against Macedon.

## CHAP. XXXVI. CLEOMENES AND THE FALL OF SPARTA.
### b.c.236–222.

Aratus cared more for Achaia than for Greece, and soon was again at war with Sparta, and Cleomenes marched out against him. He retreated, and Cleomenes in great joy put his troops in mind how in old times the Spartans never asked how many were the foe, but only where they were. Then he followed the Achaians and gained a great victory; indeed there was a doubt at first whether Aratus were not slain; but he had marched off with the remnant of the army, and next was heard of as having taken Mantinea.

This displeased the Ephors, and they called Cleomenes back. He hoped to be stronger by the aid of his fellow-king, and, as the little child of Agis had just died in his house, sent to invite home Archidamas, the brother of Agis, who was living in exile; but the Ephors had the youth murdered as soon as he reached Laconia, and then laid on Cleomenes both this murder and that of his little stepson Agis. But all the better sort held by him, and his mother Cratesiclea, and his wife Agiatis, so cleared him, that all trusted him, and he was again sent out with an army, and defeated Aratus.

He was sure he could bring back good days to Sparta, if only he were free of the Ephors. One of these, who was on his side, went to sleep in a temple, and there had a dream that four of the chairs of the Ephors were taken away, and that he heard a voice saying, "This is best for Sparta." After this, he and Cleomenes contrived that the king should lead out an army containing most of the party against him. He took them by long marches to a great distance from home, and then left them at night with a few trusty friends, with whom he fell upon the Ephors at supper, and killed four of them, the only blood he shed in this matter. In the morning he called the people together, and showed them how the Ephors had taken too much power, and how ill they had used it, especially in the murder of Agis; and the people agreed henceforth to let him rule without them. Then all debts were given up, all estates resigned to be divided again, Cleomenes himself being the first to set the example, and the partition was made. But as one line of the Heracleid kings was extinct, Cleomenes made his brother Euclidas reign with him, and was able to bring back all the old ways of Lycurgus, the hard fare and plain living, so that those who had seen the Eastern state of the upstart Macedonian soldiers wondered at the sight of the son of Hercules, descendant of a line of thirty-one kings, showing his royalty only in the noble simplicity of his bearing.

Mantinea turned out the Achaians and invited Cleomenes back, and now it was plain that the real question was whether the Spartan kingdom or the Achaian League should lead the Peloponnesus — in truth, between Aratus and Cleomenes. Another victory was gained over the Achaians, a treaty was made, and they were going to name Cleomenes head of the League, when he fell ill. He had over-tried his strength by long marches, and chilled himself by drinking cold water; he broke a blood-vessel, and had to be carried home in a litter, causing meantime the Achaian prisoners to be set free, to show that he meant to keep the treaty.

But Aratus, in his jealousy, forgot that the great work of his youth had been to get free of Macedon, and in order to put down Sparta and Cleomenes, actually asked the help of Antigonus, king of Macedon, and brought his hated troops back into the Peloponnesus, promising to welcome them, if only Cleomenes might be put down.

The brave young king had recovered and taken Argos, and soon after Corinth drove out the Achaian garrison and gave themselves to him; but the great Macedonian force under Antigonus himself was advancing, and Corinth in terror went over to him, the other allies deserted, and Cleomenes was marching back to Sparta, when a messenger met him at Tegea with tidings of the death of his beloved wife. He listened steadily, gave orders for the defence of Tegea, and then, travelling all night, went home and gave way to an agony of grief, with his mother and two little children.

He had but 5000 Spartans, and his only hope was in getting aid from Ptolemy the Benefactor, king of Egypt. This was promised, but only on condition that he would send as hostages to Egypt his mother and babes. He was exceedingly grieved, and could not bear to tell his mother; but she saw his distress, and found out the cause from his friends. She laughed in hopes of cheering him. "Was this what you feared to tell me? Put me on board ship at once, and send this old carcase where it may be of the most use to Sparta." He escorted her, at the head of the whole army, to the promontory of Tænarus, where the temple of Neptune looks out into the sea. In the temple they parted, Cleomenes weeping in such bitter sorrow that his mother's spirit rose. "Go to, king of Sparta," she said. "Without doors, let none see us weep, nor do anything contrary to the honour and dignity of Sparta. That at least is in our own power, though, for the rest, success or failure depends on the gods." So she sailed away, and Cleomenes went back to do his part. The Achaians had not only given Antigonus the title of Head of the League, but had set up his statues, and were giving him the divine honours that had been granted to Alexander and to Demetrius the City-taker.

The only part of the Peloponnesus that still held out was Laconia. Cleomenes guarded all the passes, though the struggle was almost without hope, for little help came from Egypt, only a letter from brave old Cratesiclea, begging that whatever was best for the country might be done without regard to an old woman or a child. Cleomenes then let the slaves buy their freedom, and made 2000 soldiers from among them, and marching out with these he surprised and took the Achaian city of Megalopolis. One small party of citizens, under a brave young man named Philopœmen, fought, while the rest had time to escape to Messene. Cleomenes offered to give them back the place if they would join with Sparta, but they refused, and he had the whole town plundered and burnt as a warning to the other Peloponnesians, and the next year he ravaged Argolis, and beat down the standing corn with great wooden swords.

But Antigonus had collected a vast force to subdue the Peloponnesus, and Cleomenes prepared for his last battle at Sellasia, a place between two hills. On one named Evas he placed his brother Euclidas, on the other named Olympus he posted himself, with his cavalry in the middle. He had but 20,000 men, and Antigonus three times as many, with all the Achaians among them. Euclidas did not, as his brother had intended, charge down the hill, but was driven backwards over the precipices that lay behind him. The cavalry were beaten by Philopœmen, who fought all day, though a javelin had pierced both his legs; and Cleomenes found it quite impossible to break the Macedonian phalanx, and out of his 6000 Spartans found himself at the end of the day with only 200.

With these he rode back to Sparta, where he stopped in the market-place to tell his people that all was lost, and they had better make what terms they could. They should decide whether his life or death were best for him, and while they deliberated, he turned towards his own empty house, but he could not bear to enter it. A slave girl taken from Megalopolis ran out to bring him food and drink, but he would taste nothing, only being tired out he leant his arm sideways against a pillar and laid his head on it, and so he waited in silence till word was brought him that the citizens wished him to escape.

He quietly left Sparta and sailed for Alexandria, where the king, Ptolemy the Benefactor, at first was short and cold with him, because he would not cringe to him, but soon learned to admire him, treated him as a brother, promised him help to regain Sparta, and gave him a pension, which he spent in relieving other exiled Greeks. But the Benefactor died, and his son, Ptolemy Philopator, was a selfish wretch, who hated and dreaded the grave, stern man who was a continual rebuke to him, and who, the Alexandrians said, walked about like a lion in a sheepfold. He refused the fleet his father had promised, would not let Cleomenes go back alone to try his fortune on Antigonus' death, and at last, on some report of his meaning to attack Cyrene, had him shut up with his friends in a large room. They broke forth, and tried to fight their way to a ship, but they were hemmed in, no one came to their aid, and rather than be taken prisoners, they all fell on their own swords; and on the tidings, Ptolemy commanded all the women and children to be put to death. Cratesiclea saw her two grandsons slain before her eyes, and then crying, "Oh, children, where are ye gone?" herself held out her neck for the rope.

TEMPLE OF NEPTUNE.

## CHAP. XXXVII. PHILOPŒMEN, THE LAST OF THE GREEKS.
### b.c. 236–184.

The jealousy and rivalry of Aratus and the Achaians had made them put themselves under the power of Macedon, in order thus to overthrow Sparta. Aratus seemed to have lost all his skill and spirit, for when the robber Ætolians again made an attack on the Peloponnesus, he managed so ill as to have a great defeat; and the Achaians were forced again to call for the help of the Macedonians, whose king was now Philip, son to Antigonus.

A war went on for many years between the Macedonians, with the Achaians on the one hand and the Ætolians on the other. Aratus was a friend and adviser to Philip, but would gladly have loosened the yoke he had helped to lay on Greece. When the old Messenian town of Ithome fell into the hands of Philip, he went into the temple of Jupiter, with Aratus and another adviser called Demetrius the Pharian, to consult the sacrifices as to whether he should put a garrison into Ithome to overawe Messenia. The omens were doubtful, and Philip asked his two friends what they thought. Demetrius said, "If you have the soul of a priest, you will restore the fort to the Messenians; if you have the soul of a prince, you will hold the ox by both his horns."

The ox was, of course, the Peloponnesus, and the other horn was the Acro-Corinthus, which, with Ithome, gave Philip power over the whole peninsula. The king then asked Aratus' advice. He said, "Thieves nestle in the fastnesses of rocks. A king's best fortress is loyalty and love;" and at his words Philip turned away, and left the fort to its own people. He was at that time a youth full of good promise, but he let himself be led astray by the vices and pleasures of his court, and withdrew his favour from Aratus. Then he began to misuse the

Messenians, and had their country ravaged. Aratus, who was for the seventeenth time general of the League, made a complaint, and Philip, in return, contrived that he should be slowly poisoned. He said nothing; only once, when a friend noticed his illness, he said, "This is the effect of the friendship of kings." He died in 213, and just about this time Philopœmen of Megalopolis returned from serving in the Cretan army to fight for his country. He was a thoroughly noble-hearted man, and a most excellent general, and he did much to improve the Achaian army. In the meantime Sparta had fallen under the power of another tyrant, called Nabis, a horribly cruel wretch, who had had a statue made in the likeness of his wife, with nails and daggers all over her breast. His enemies were put into her arms; she clasped them, and thus they died. He robbed the unhappy people of Sparta; and all the thieves, murderers, and outlaws of the country round were taken into his service, and parties of them sent out to collect plunder all over the Peloponnesus. At last one of his grooms ran away with some horses, and took refuge at Megalopolis, and this Nabis made a cause for attacking both that city and Messenia; but at last Philopœmen was made general of the Achaian League, and gave the wretch such a defeat as forced him to keep at home, while Philopœmen ravaged Laconia.

Philip of Macedon offered to come and drive out Nabis if the Achaians would help him, but they distrusted him, and did not choose to go to war with the Romans, whom the robber Ætolians had called from Italy to assist them. However, Philip reduced Nabis to make all sorts of promises and treaties, which, of course, he did not keep, but invited in the Ætolians to assist him. This, however, brought his punishment on him, for soon after their arrival these allies of his murdered him, and began to rob all Laconia. Philopœmen and his Achaians at once marched into the country, helped the Spartans to deliver themselves from the robbers, and persuaded them to join the League. They were so much pleased with him that they resolved to give him Nabis' palace and treasure, but he was known to hate bribes so much that nobody could at first be found to make him the offer. One man was sent to Megalopolis, but when he saw Philopœmen's plain, grave, hardy life, and heard how much he disapproved of sloth and luxury, he did not venture to say a word about the palace full of Eastern magnificence, but went back to Sparta. He was sent again, and still found no opportunity; and when, the third time, he did speak, Philopœmen thanked the Spartans, but said he advised them not to spend their riches on spoiling honest men, whose help they might have at no cost at all, but rather to use them in buying over those who made mischief among them.

Wars were going on at this time between Philip of Macedon, on the one side, and the Ætolians on the other. Philip's ally was Antiochus the Great, the Greek king of Syria; the Ætolians had called in the Romans, that great, conquering Italian nation, whose plan was always to take the part of some small nation against a more powerful one, break the strength of both, and then join them to their own empire. But the Achaians did not know this, and wished them well, while they defeated the Macedonians at the great battle of Cynocephalæ, or the Dog's Head Rocks, in Thessaly. Philip was obliged to make peace, and one condition required of him was that he should give up all claims to power over Greece. Then at Corinth, at the Isthmian games, the Roman consul, Quintius Flaminius, proclaimed that the Greek states were once more free. Such a shout of joy was raised that it is said that birds flying in the air overhead dropped down with the shock, and Flaminius was almost stifled by the crowds of grateful Greeks who came round him to cover him with garlands and kiss his hands.

CROWNING THE VICTOR IN THE ISTHMIAN GAMES.

But, after all, the Romans meant to keep a hold on Greece, though they left the cities to themselves for a little while. The Spartans who had been banished by Nabis had not returned home, but lived a life of robbery, which was thought to be favoured by Philopœmen, and this offended those at home, some of whom plundered a town called Las. The Achaians demanded that the guilty should be given up to them for punishment, and a war began, which ended by a savage attack on Sparta, in which Philopœmen forgot all but the old enmity between Achaia and Laconia, put ninety citizens to death, pulled down the walls, besides abolishing the laws of Lycurgus, which, however, nobody had observed since the fall of Cleomenes. Many citizens were sent into banishment, and these went to Rome to complain of the Achaians. While they were gone the Messenians rose against the League, while Philopœmen was lying sick of a fever at Argos; but though he was ill, and seventy years old, he collected a small troop of young Megalopolitan horsemen, to join the main army with them. But he met the full force of the Messenians, and while fighting bravely to shelter his young followers, received a blow on the head which stunned him, so that he was made prisoner, and carried to Messene. There his enemies showed him in the theatre, but the people only recollected how noble he was, and how he had defended all Greece from Nabis. So his enemies hurried him away, and put him in an underground dungeon, where, at night, they sent an executioner to carry him a dose of poison. Philopœmen raised himself with difficulty, for he was very weak, and asked the man whether he could tell him what had become of his young Megalopolitan friends. The man replied that he thought they had most of them escaped. "You bring good news," said Philopœmen; then, swallowing the draught, he laid himself on his back, and, almost instantly died. He is called the Last of the Greeks, for there never was a great man of the old sort after him.

LIVADIA, THE ANCIENT MIDEIA IN ARGOLIS.

## CHAP. XXXVIII. — THE FALL OF GREECE. b.c. 189-146.

After the death of Philopœmen there was little real spirit left in the Achaians, and Callicrates, who became the leading man among them, led them to submit themselves to the senate of Rome, and do as it pleased with regard to Sparta and Messene.

Philip of Macedon was at war with Rome all his life, and his son Perseus went on with it. Marcus Paullus Æmilius, one of the best and bravest of the Romans, was sent to subdue him, and the great battle was fought in 188, at Pydna, near Mount Olympus. The night before the battle there was an eclipse of the moon, which greatly terrified the Macedonians; but the Romans had among them an officer who knew enough of the movements of the heavenly bodies to have told the soldiers of it beforehand, and its cause. The Macedonians being thus discouraged, gave way, and fled as soon as the battle seemed to be going against them; and Perseus himself galloped from the field to Pella, where he was so beside himself with despair that he stabbed two of his counsellors who tried to show him the mistakes he had made. But as Æmilius advanced, he was forced to retreat before him, even into the island of Samothrace, which was sacred soil, whence he could not be taken by force. The Romans watched all round the island, and he dreaded that the Samothracians should give him up to them; so he bargained with a Cretan shipmaster to take him and all his treasure on board his ship, and carry him off at night. The Cretan received half the treasure, and Perseus crept out at a small window, crossed a garden, and reached the wharf, where, to his horror, he found that the treacherous captain had sailed off with the treasure, and left him behind.

There was nothing for him to do but to yield to the Romans. He came into the camp in mourning, and Æmilius gave him his hand and received him kindly, but kept him a prisoner, and formed Macedon into a province under Roman government. Æmilius himself went on a journey through the most famous Greek cities, especially admiring Athens, and looking at the places made famous by historians, poets, and philosophers. He took Polybius, a learned Athenian philosopher, who wrote the history of this war, to act as tutor to his two sons, though both were young men able to fight in this campaign, and from that time forward the Romans were glad to have Greek teachers for their sons, and Greek was spoken by them as freely and easily as their own Latin; every well-educated man knew the chief Greek poets by heart, and was of some school of philosophy, either Stoic or Epicurean, but the best men were generally Stoics.

SAPPHO.

Perseus and his two young sons were taken to Rome, there, according to the Roman fashion, to march in the triumph of the conqueror, namely, the procession in which the general returned home with all his troops. It was a shame much feared by the conquered princes, and the cruel old rule was that they should be put to death at the close of the march. Paullus Æmilius was, however, a man of kind temper, and had promised Perseus to spare his life. The unfortunate king begged to be spared the humiliation of walking in the triumph, but Æmilius could not disappoint the Roman people, and answered that "the favour was in Perseus' own power," meaning, since he knew no better, that to die should prevent what was so much dreaded. Perseus, however, did not take the counsel, but lived in an Italian city for the rest of his life.

After Macedon was ruined the Romans resolved to put down all stirrings of resistance to them in the rest of Greece. Their friend Callicrates, therefore, accused all the Achaians who had been friendly to Perseus, or who had any brave spirit — 1000 in number — of conspiring against Rome, and called on the League to sentence them to death; but as this proposal was heard with horror, they were sent to Rome to justify themselves, and the Roman senate, choosing to suppose they had been judged by the League, sentenced them never to return to Achaia. Polybius was among them, so that his home was thenceforth in the house of his pupils, the sons of Æmilius. Many times did the Achaians send entreaties that they might be set at liberty, and at last, after seventeen years, Polybius' pupils persuaded the great senator Cato to speak for them, and he did so, but in a very rough, unfeeling way. "Anyone who saw us disputing whether a set of poor old Greeks should be buried by our grave-diggers or their own would think we had nothing else to do," he said. So the Romans consented to their going home; but when they asked to have all their rank and honours restored to them, Cato said, "Polybius, you are less wise than Ulysses. You want to go back into the Cyclops' cave for the wretched rags and tatters you left behind you there." After all, Polybius either did not go home or did not stay there, for he was soon again with his beloved pupils; and in the seventeen years of exile the 1000 had so melted away that only 300 went home again.

LESSINA, THE ANCIENT ELEUSIS, ON THE GULF OF CORINTH.

But the very year after their return a fresh rising was made by the Macedonians, under a pretender who claimed to be the son of Perseus, and by the Peloponnesians, with the Achaians and Spartans at their head, while the Corinthians insulted the Roman ambassadors. A Roman general named Quintus Metellus was sent to subdue them, and routed the Macedonians at the battle of Scarphæa, but after that another general named Mummius was sent out. The Achaians had collected all their strength against him, and in the first skirmish gained a little success; and this encouraged them to risk a battle, in which they were so confident of victory that they placed their wives and children on a hill to watch them, and provided waggons to carry away the spoil. The battle was fought at Leucoptera, near the Isthmus, and all this boasting was soon turned into a miserable defeat. Diæus, who commanded the Greeks, was put to flight, and riding off to Megalopolis in utter despair, he killed his wife and children, to prevent their falling into the hands of the enemy, and then poisoned himself.

The other Achaians at first retreated into Corinth, and in the course of the night scattered themselves each to his own city. In the morning Mummius marched in and gave up the unhappy city to plunder. All the men were slain, all the women and children taken for slaves, and when all the statues, pictures, and jewels had been gathered out of the temples and houses, the place was set on fire, and burnt unceasingly for several days; the walls were pulled down, and the city blotted out from Greece. There was so much metal of all kinds in the burning houses that it all became fused together, and produced a new and valuable metal called Corinthian brass. The Romans were at this time still very rude and ignorant, and did not at all understand the value and beauty of the works of art they carried off. Polybius saw two soldiers making a dice-board of one of the most famous pictures in Greece; and Mummius was much laughed at for telling the captains of the ships who took home some of the statues to exhibit in his triumph that if they lost them they should supply new ones at their own cost. The Corinthians suffered thus for having insulted the ambassadors. The other cities submitted without a blow, and were left untouched to govern themselves, but in subjection to Rome, and with Roman garrisons in their citadels. Polybius was sent round them to assure them of peace, and they had it for more than 500 years, but the freedom of Greece was gone for ever.

## CHAP. XXXIX. — THE GOSPEL IN GREECE. b.c. 146–a.d. 60.

After a time Macedon and Achaia were made by the Romans into provinces, each of which had a governor who had been one year in a magistrate's office at Rome, and then was sent out to rule in a province for three or for five years.

In 146, nearly a hundred years after the ruin of Corinth, Julius Cæsar built it up again in great strength and beauty, and made it the capital of Achaia. As it stood where the Isthmus was only six miles across, and had a beautiful harbour on each side, travellers who did not wish to go round the dangerous headlands of the Peloponnesus used to land on one side and embark on the other. Thus Corinth become one of the great stations for troops, and also a mart for all kinds of merchandise, and was always full of strangers, both Greeks and Jews.

The Romans, as conquerors, had rights to be tried only by their own magistrates and laws, and these laws were generally just. They were, however, very hard on subject nations; and, therefore, the best thing that could happen to a man was to be made a Roman citizen, and this was always done to persons of rank, by way of compliment — sometimes to whole cities.

VIEW FROM CORINTH.

Athens had never had a great statesman or soldier in her since the time of Phocion, but her philosophers and orators still went on discoursing in the schools, and for four hundred years at least Athens was a sort of university town, where the rich young men from Rome, Carthage, Alexandria, Asia Minor, and Syria came to see the grand old buildings and works of art, and to finish their education. For though the great men of Greece were all dead, their works, both in stone and in writing, still remained, and were the models of all the world, and their language was spoken all over the East. The Romans' own tongue, Latin, was used at home, of course, but every gentleman knew Greek equally well, and all the Syrians, Jews, and Egyptians who had much intercourse with them used Greek as the language sure to be known — much as French is now used all over Europe.

But there was an answer coming to all those strainings and yearnings after God and His truth which had made those old Greek writings beautiful. There is a story that one night a ship's crew, passing near a lonely island in the Ægean Sea, sacred to the gods, heard a great wailing and crying aloud of spirit voices, exclaiming, "Great Pan is dead."

Pan was the heathen god of nature, to whom sacred places were dedicated, and this strange crying was at the very night after a day when, far away in Judæa, the sun had been darkened at noon, and the rocks were rent, and One who was dying on a cross had said, "It is finished." For the victory over Satan and all his spirits was won by death.

Some fifteen years later than that day, as Paul, a Jew of Tarsus, in Asia Minor, with the right of Roman citizenship, and a Greek education, was spreading the knowledge of that victory over the East — while he slept at the new Troy built by Alexander, there stood by his bed, in a vision by night, a man of Macedon, saying, "Come over and help us."

He went, knowing that the call came from God, and the cities of Macedon gained quite new honours. Philippi, where he was first received, had a small number of Jews in it, to whom he spake by the river side, but many Greeks soon began to listen; and then it was that the evil spirits, who spake aloud to men in heathen lands, first had to own the power of Christ, who had conquered. A slave girl, who had long been possessed by one of these demons, was forced at the sight of Paul and his companion Silas to cry aloud, "These men are the servants of the Most High God, which show unto us the way of salvation." She followed them about for some days doing this, until Paul, grieved in the spirit, bade the evil one, in JESUS' name, to leave her. At once the name of the Conqueror caused the demon to depart; but the owner of the slave girl, enraged at the loss of her soothsaying powers, accused the Apostle and his friend to the magistrates, and, without examination, they were thrown into prison. At night, while they sang praise in the dungeon, an earthquake shook it; the doors were open, the fetters loosed, and the jailer, thinking them fled, would have killed himself, but for Paul's call to him that all were safe. He heard the Word of life that night, and was baptised; but St. Paul would not leave the prison, either then or at the permission of the magistrates, when they found they had exceeded their powers, but insisted that they should come themselves to fetch him out, thus marking his liberty as a Roman, so that others might fear to touch him. He had founded a church at Philippi, in which he always found great comfort and joy; and when he was forced to go on to Thessalonica, he found many willing and eager hearers among the Greeks; but the Jews, enraged at his teaching these, stirred up the mob, and not only forced him to leave that city, but hunted him wherever he tried to stop in Macedon, so that he was obliged to hurry into the next province, Achaia, and wait at Athens for the companions whom he had left to go on with his work at Philippi and Thessalonica.

PARTHENON AND ERECTHEUM.

While at Athens, the multitude of altars and temples, and the devotion paid to them, stirred his spirit, so that he could not but speak out plainly, and point to the truth. It seemed a new philosophy to the talkers and inquirers, who had talked to shreds the old arguments of Plato and Epicurus, and longed for some fresh light or new interest; and he was invited to Areopagus to set forth his doctrine. There, in the face of the Parthenon and the Acropolis, with philosophers and students from all parts of the empire around, he made one of his greatest and noblest speeches — "Ye men of Athens, I perceive that in all things ye are greatly religious. For as I passed through your city, and beheld how ye worship, I found an altar with this inscription — 'TO THE UNKNOWN GOD.' Whom, therefore, ye ignorantly worship; Him declare I unto you."

Then, looking forth on the temples crowded on the rocks, he tried to open their minds to the truth that the God of all dwells in no temples made with hands, that all men alike are His children, and that, since living, breathing, thinking man has sprung from Him, it is lowering His greatness to represent Him by cold, dead, senseless stone, metal, or ivory. "He bore with the times of ignorance," said Paul; "but now He called on all men to turn to Him to prepare for the day when

212

all should be judged, by the Man whom He had ordained for the purpose, as had been shown by His rising from the dead."

The Greeks had listened to the proclamation of one great unseen God, higher than art could represent; but when Paul spoke of rising from the dead, they burst into mockery. They had believed in spirits living, but not in bodies rising again, and the philosophers would not listen. Very few converts were made in Athens, only Dionysius, and a woman named Damaris, and a few more; and the city of learning long closed her ears against those who would have taught her what Socrates and Plato had been feeling after like men in the dark.

At the merchant city of Corinth, Paul had greater success; he stayed there nearly two years, and from thence sent letters to the Thessalonians, who were neglecting their daily duties, expecting that our Lord was about immediately to return. After Paul had left Corinth, he wrote to that city also, first to correct certain evils that had arisen in the Church there, and afterwards to encourage those who had repented, and promise another visit. This visit, as well as one to his Macedonian churches, was paid in his third journey; and when he had been arrested at Jerusalem, and was in Rome awaiting his trial before the emperor, Nero, he wrote to his friends at Philippi what is called the Epistle of Joy, so bright were his hopes of his friends there.

St. Andrew also laboured in Greece, and was put to death in Achaia, by being fastened to a cross of olive-wood, shaped like an X, where he hung exhorting the people for three days before he died. When St. Paul was released, he and the great evangelist St. John, and such of the apostles as still survived, set the Church in order, appointing bishops over their cities, and Dionysius of Athens became Bishop of Corinth, and St. Paul's pupil from Antioch, Titus, was Bishop of Crete, and received an epistle from Paul on the duties of his office. In process of time Christianity won its way, and the oracles became silent, as the demons which spoke in them fled from the Name of JESUS.

DISTANT VIEW OF PARNASSUS.

## CHAP. XL. — UNDER THE ROMAN EMPIRE.

For three hundred years Rome reigned over all the countries round the Mediterranean, with one emperor at her head, and the magistrates of his appointment to rule in all the provinces, while garrisons were placed to quell risings of the people, or to keep in order the wild tribes on any dangerous border. For a long course of years Greece was quiet, and had no need of such troops. The people of her cities were allowed to manage their own affairs enough to satisfy them and make them contented, though they had lost all but such freedom as they could have by being enrolled as citizens of Rome, and they were too near the heart of the empire to be in danger from barbarous neighbours, so that they did not often have troops among them, except those passing through Corinth to the East.

Towards the end of these three hundred years, however, Thrace and Thessaly began to be threatened by wild nations who came from the banks of the Danube, and robbed the rich villages and countries to the south. The empire was, in truth, growing weaker, and enemies began to press upon it; and this made the emperor, Diocletian, decide that it was beyond the power of any one man to rule and defend it all, and he therefore divided it with his friend Maximian, whom he made Emperor of the East, while he remained Emperor of the West. The Western empire was the Latin-speaking half, and the Eastern the Greek-speaking half, of these lands, though both still called themselves Roman.

PLAINS OF PHILIPPI.

The two halves were joined together again, about the year 300, under Constantine the Great, who was the first Christian emperor. He thought he should be more in the middle of his government if he moved his capital from Rome to the old Greek city of Byzantium, which he adorned with most splendid buildings, and called after his own name, Constantinople; and this became the capital of the East, as Rome was of the West. Athens remained all this time the place of study for Christians as well as heathens, and people still talked philosophy and studied eloquence among the laurel and myrtle groves, and looked at the temples, which still stood there, though hardly anyone frequented them. One emperor, Julian, the cousin of Constantine, studied there as a youth, and became so fond of the old philosophy and learning, and so admired the noble ways of the times when men were seeking after truth, that he thought Greece and Rome would be great again if they turned back to these heathen ways, not seeing that this was going back to the dark out of which those men had been struggling.

Julian tried to bring back heathen customs, and to have the old gods worshipped again; but he was killed in an expedition against the Persians, and soon after his time the old idol-worship was quite forgotten. Every city had a Bishop and clergy, and the Bishops of each division of the empire were under a great ruling Bishop, who was called a Patriarch. Greece was under the Patriarch of Constantinople. The Greek churches were made as like the pattern of the temple at Jerusalem as they could be. The end which represented the Holy of Holies, and had the altar in it, was veiled, and enclosed within what were called the Royal Gates, and these were only opened at times of celebrating the Holy Communion. This end was raised steps, and the Holy Scriptures and sermon were spoken to the people from the front of the Royal Gates. The pavement was of rich marble, and the ceiling, which was generally vaulted, was inlaid with coloured stones, making pictures in what is called Mosaic, because thus the stones were set by Moses in the High Priest's vestment. The clergy wore robes like those of the priests, and generally had flowing hair and beards, though in front the hair was cut in a circlet, in memory of our Lord's crown of thorns.

Now that everyone had become Christian, and bad or worldly people were not afraid to belong to the Church for fear of persecution, there was often sin and evil among them. Many who grieved at this shut themselves up from the world in the most lonely places they could find — little islands, deep woods, mountain tops, or rocks, and the like. When they lived alone they were called hermits, when there were many together they were called monks, and the women who thus lived were nuns. Many such monasteries there were in Greece, especially one upon Mount Athos — that peninsula that Xerxes tried to cut off — and most of these have continued even to our own time.

The emperor Theodosius, who reigned at the end of this fourth century over both East and West, was a very good and great man, and during his reign the Greek lands were kept from the marauders. In his time, however, the Thessalonians brought a most dreadful punishment on themselves. For want of public business, or any real and noble interest, the people had come to care for nothing but games and races, and they loved these sports with a sort of passionate fury. There was a chariot-driver at Thessalonica who was a wicked man, but whose racing was so much admired that when, for some crime, Botheric, the governor, put him in prison and hindered his performance, the mob rose, when they missed him in the amphitheatre, and threw stones at the governor and his officers, so that several were killed, and Botheric among them. The news was taken to the emperor, and in great wrath he ordered that the Thessalonians should be punished. The order was given to a cruel, savage man, who hurried off at once, lest the emperor should relent and stop him. He invited the Thessalonians to meet him in the amphitheatre, and when they were there, expecting to hear some message, he had all the doors closed, and sent in his soldiers, who killed them all, innocent as well as guilty, even strangers who had only just come to the place.

Theodosius was much shocked to find how his passionate words had been obeyed, and the good Bishop of Milan, St. Ambrose, made him wait as a penitent, cut off from the Holy Communion, while he was thus stained with blood, until after many months his repentance could be accepted, and he could be forgiven.

OBELISK OF THEODOSIUS, CONSTANTINOPLE.

After Theodosius died, the Western half of the empire was overrun and conquered by tribes of German nations, but the Eastern part still remained, and emperor after emperor reigned at Constantinople, ruling over the Greek cities as before; but there were savage tribes of the Slavonian race who settled in Thrace, and spread over Thessaly. They were called Bulgarians, and used to send marauders all over the country to the south, so that they were much dreaded by the Greeks, who had long forgotten how to fight for themselves.

But though the Eastern and Western empires were broken apart, the Church was one. The Greeks, indeed, found fault with the Romans for putting three words into the Creed of Nicea which had not been decided on by the consent of the whole Church in Council, and there was a question between the Pope of Rome and the Patriarch of Constantinople as to which had the chief rule. At last their disputes in the eleventh century caused a schism, or ruling apart, and the Greek Church became separated from the Roman Church.

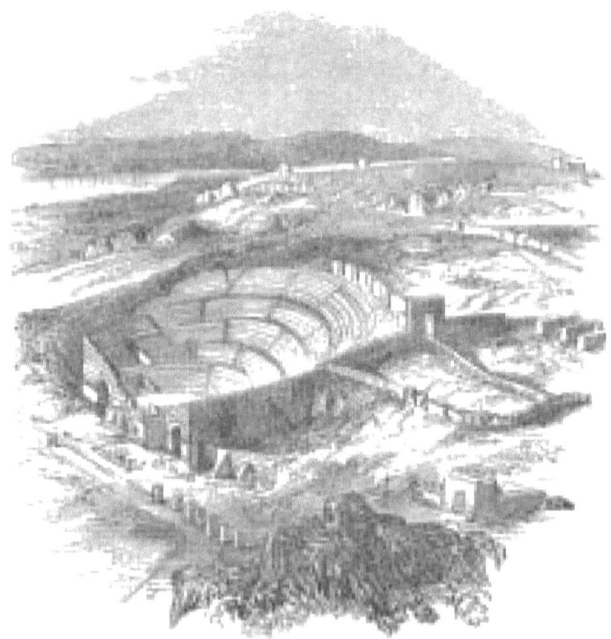

AN AMPHITHEATRE-SEE PAGE 312.

## CHAP. XLI. — THE FRANK CONQUEST. 1201-1446.

There is very little to tell about Greece for hundreds of years. It was a part of the Eastern Empire, and was for the most part in a quiet state, except when robbers came against it. The Bulgarians came from the North, but after they had become Christian they were somewhat less dangerous. From the East and South came Saracens and Moors, who had been converted to the faith of the false Arabian prophet Mahommed; and from the West came the Northmen, all the way from Norway and Denmark, to rob the very east end of the Mediterranean, so that beautiful old ornaments, evidently made in Greece, have been found in the northern homes that once belonged to these sea-kings.

The Greeks had little spirit to fight, and the emperors took some of these stout Northmen into their pay against the Bulgarians and Saracens, calling them their Varangian Guard. Another band, of northern blood, though they had been settled in Normandy for two generations, came, and after driving out the Saracens from Sicily and Southern Italy, set up two little kingdoms there. Robert Guiscard, or the Wizard, the first and cleverest of these Norman kings, had a great wish to gain Greece also, and had many fights with the troops of the Emperor of the East, Alexis Comnenus. Their quarrels with him made the Greeks angry and terrified when all the bravest men of the West wanted to come through their lands on the Crusade, or Holy War, to deliver Jerusalem from the Saracens. Then, since the schism between the Churches, the Greeks and the Latins had learnt scarcely to think of one another as Christians at all, and certainly they did not behave to one another like Christians, for the Greeks cunningly robbed, harassed, and deceived the Latins, and the Latins were harsh, rude, and violent with the Greeks.

In the northern point of the Adriatic Sea lay the city of Venice, built upon a cluster of little islands. The people had taken refuge there when Italy was overrun by the barbarians. In course of time these Venetians had grown to be a mighty and powerful people, whose merchant ships traded all over the Mediterranean, and whose counsellors were famed for wisdom. They had shaken off the power of the Greek emperor, and were governed by a senate and council, with a chosen nobleman at its head, who was called the Doge, or Duke. Just when the French, Germans, and Italians were setting off on the Fourth Crusade, in the year 1201, meaning to sail in Venetian ships, the young Alexius Angelus, son to the emperor Isaac Angelus, came to beg for help for his poor old father, who had been thrown into prison by his own brother, with his eyes put out. It was quite aside from the main work of the Crusade, but the Venetians had always had a quarrel with the Greek emperors, and they prevailed to turn the army aside to attack Constantinople. With an immense pair of shears they cut in twain the great chains which shut in the harbour of the Golden Horn, and sailed safely in, led by their Doge, Dandolo, who, though eighty years old, and blind, was as keen on the battle as the youngest man there.

The French scaled the walls, the usurper fled, and blind old Isaac was led out of his dungeon, and dressed in his robes again; his son was crowned to reign with him, and they did everything to please the Crusaders. Chiefly they made the Patriarch of Constantinople consent to give up all the differences with the Roman Catholic Church, and own the Pope as superior to him. This made the Greeks angry, and they could not bear to see their young emperor so familiar with the French knights, whom they looked on as barbarians. One day he was seen with a Frenchman's cap on his head, and his own crown lying on the ground at his feet. In great anger the people of Constantinople rose, under a man named Alexius Ducas, called "Black-brows," murdered the two emperors, and set up this new one; but he did not reign long, for the French and Venetians were close at hand. There was a second siege, and when the city was taken they plundered it throughout, stripped it of all the wealth they could collect, and set up Baldwin, Count of Flanders, to be emperor, with a Latin Patriarch; while the Venetians helped themselves to all the southern part of the empire, namely, the Peloponnesus and the Greek islands; and a French nobleman named Walter de Brienne was created Duke of Athens, under the Flemish emperor.

PROMONTORY OF ACTIUM.

It was then that so many of the old Greek places took the names we now see them called by in the map, and which were mostly given by the Venetian seamen. They called the Peloponnesus the Morea, or Mulberry-leaf, because it was in that shape; they called the island of Eubœa, Negropont, or Black-bridge; the Ægean Sea, the Archipelago, or Great Sea; and the Euxine, the Black Sea, because it is so dangerous. The Greeks hated their new masters very much, and would not conform to the Roman Catholic Church. A new Greek empire was set up in Asia Minor, at Nicea; and after the Latin emperor Baldwin had been lost in a battle with the Bulgarians, and great troubles swept away his successors, the emperors returned to Constantinople, under Michael Palæologus, in 1261, and drove out all the Franks, as the Greeks called the Western people, chiefly French and Italians, who had come to settle in their cities.

But the Venetians still held the cities in the greater part of the Morea, and some of the islands, and traded all over the East and West, though their Greek subjects were only kept under by main force, still held to their own Greek Church, and looked to the Roman Emperor of the East, as they called the Palæologus at Constantinople, as their head; nor was it easy to overpower people who had so many mountain fastnesses, nor to tame monks whose convents were nests on the top of rocks, some so steep that there was no way of entering them save being drawn up in a basket. Well was it for them that they had niched themselves into such strongholds, for worse and worse days were coming upon Greece. The terrible nation of Turks were making their way out of the wild country north of Persia, and winning the old cities of Asia Minor, where they set up their Mahommedan dominion, and threatened more and more to overthrow the Greek empire altogether.

The emperor, John Palæologus, was obliged to yield to Amurath, the Turkish Sultan, all his lands except Constantinople, Thessalonica, and that part of the Morea which still clung to the empire, and the Turks set up their capital at Adrianople, whence they spread their conquests up to the very walls of Constantinople; but the Greek mountaineers, especially those of the mountain land of Epirus, now called Albania, had something of the old spirit among them, and fought hard. The Venetians used to take troops of them into their pay, since all Christians made common cause against the Turks; and these soldiers, richly armed, with white Albanian kilts, the remnant of the old Greek tunic, were called Stradiots, from the old Greek word for a soldier, Stratiotes. The bravest of them all was George Castriotes, a young Albanian, who had been given as a hostage to the Mahommedans when nine years old. He had been kept a prisoner, and made to fight in the Turkish army, and was so brave there that the Turks called him Skanderbeg, or the Lord Alexander. However, when he thought of the horror of being a Mahommedan, and fighting against the Christian faith and his own country, he fled into Albania, raised all the Greeks, killed all the Turks in the country, and kept it safe from all the further attempts of the Sultan as long as he lived, although, at Varna, a great crusade of all the most adventurous spirits in Europe, to drive back the Turks, was wofully defeated in the year 1446.

MOUNT HELICON.

## CHAP. XLII. — THE TURKISH CONQUEST. 1453–1670.

The last Emperor of the East was the best and bravest who had reigned for many years. Constantine Palæologus did his best against the Turks, but Mahommed II., one of the greatest of the Ottoman race, was Sultan, and vowed that Constantinople should be either his throne or his tomb.

When the besieged Christians heard the Turks outside their walls chanting their prayers, they knew that the city would be assaulted the next day, and late at night Constantine called his friends together, and said, "Though my heart is full, I can speak to you no longer. There is the crown which I hold from God. I place it in your hands; I entrust it to you. I fight to deserve it still, or to die in defending it." They wept and wailed so that he had to wait to be heard again, and then he said, "Comrades, this is our fairest day;" after which they all went to the Cathedral of St. Sophia, and received the Holy Communion together. There was a crowd around as he came out, and he stood before them, begging them to pardon him for not having been able to make them happier. They answered with sobs and tears, and then he mounted his horse and rode round the defences.

CATHEDRAL OF ST. SOPHIA.

The Turks began the attack in the early morning, and the fight raged all day; but they were the most numerous, and kept thronging into the breach, so that, though Constantine fought like a lion at bay, he could not save the place, and the last time his voice was heard it was crying out, "Is there no Christian who will cut off my head?" The Turks pressed in on all sides, cut down the Christians, won street after street, house after house; and when at last Mahommed rode up to the palace where Roman emperors had reigned for 1100 years, he was so much struck with the desolation that he repeated a verse of Persian poetry —

"The spider hath woven her web in the palace of kings,
The owl hath sung her watch-song in the towers of Afrasiab."

Search was made for the body of Constantine, and it was found under a heap of slain, sword in hand, and so much disfigured that it was only known by the golden eagles worked on his buskins. The whole city fell under the Turks, and the nobles and princes in the mountains of the Morea likewise owned Mahommed as their sovereign. Only Albania held out as long as the brave Skanderbeg lived to guard it; but at last, in 1466, he fell ill of a fever, and finding that he should not live, he called his friends and took leave of them, talking over the toils they had shared. In the midst there was an alarm that the Turks were making an inroad, and the smoke of the burning villages could be seen. George called for his armour, and tried to rise, but he was too weak, so he bade his friends hasten to the defence, saying he should soon be able to follow. When the Turks saw his banner, they thought he must be there, and fled, losing many men in the narrow mountain roads; but the Greeks had only just brought back the news of their success, when their great leader died. His horse loved him so much that it would not allow itself to be touched by any other person, became wild and fierce, and died in a few weeks' time. The Albanians could not hold out long without their gallant chief; and when the Turks took Alyssio, the body of Castriotes was taken from its grave, and the bones were divided among his enemies, who wore them as charms in cases of gold and silver, fancying they would thus gain a share of his bravery.

The Turkish empire thus included all Greece on the mainland, but the Greeks were never really subdued. On all the steep hills were castles or convents, which the Turks were unable to take; and though there were Turkish Beys and Pashas, with soldiers placed in the towns to overawe the people, and squeeze out a tribute, and a great deal more besides, from the Greek tradesmen and farmers, the main body of the people still remembered they were Greeks and Christians. Each village had its own church and priest, each diocese its bishop, all subject to the Patriarchs of Constantinople; and the Sultans, knowing what power these had over the minds of the people, kept them always closely watched, often imprisoned them, and sometimes put them to death. The islands for the most part were still under Venice, and some of the braver-spirited young men became Stradiots in the Venetian service; but too many only went off into the mountains, and became robbers and outlaws there, while those who lived a peaceable life gave way under their miseries to the two greatest faults there had always been in the Greek nature, namely, cheating and lying. They were so sharp and clever that the dull Turks were forced to employ them, so that they grew rich fast; and then, as soon as the Pasha suspected them of having wealth, however poor they seemed to be, he would seize them, rob them, or kill them to get their money; and, what was worse, their daughters were taken away to be slaves or wives to these Mahommedans. The clergy could get little teaching, and grew as rude and ignorant as their flocks; for though the writings of the great teachers of the early Church were laid up in the libraries in the convents, nobody ever touched them. But just as, after the Macedonian conquest of old Greece, the language spread all over the East; so, after the Turkish conquest of Constantinople, Greek became much better known in Europe, for many learned men of the schools of Constantinople took refuge in Italy, bringing their books with them; the scholars eagerly learned Greek, and the works of Homer and of the great old Greek tragedians became more and more known, and were made part of a learned education. The Greeks at home still spoke the old tongue, though it had become as much altered from that of Athens and Sparta as Italian is from Latin.

The most prosperous time of all the Turkish power was under Solyman the Magnificent, who spread his empire from the borders of Hungary to those of Persia, and held in truth nearly the same empire as Alexander the Great. He conquered the island of Rhodes, on the Christmas day of 1522, from the Knights of St. John, who were Frankish monks sworn to fight against the Mahommedans. Cyprus belonged to the Venetians, and in 1571 a Jew, who had renounced his faith, persuaded Sultan Selim to have it attacked, that he might gain his favourite Cyprus wine for the pressing, instead of buying it. The Venetian stores of gunpowder had been blown up by an accident, and they could not send help in time to the unfortunate governor, who was made prisoner, and treated with most savage cruelty. However, fifty years later, in 1571, the powers of Europe joined together under Don John of Austria, the brother of the king of Spain, and beat the Turks in a great sea-fight at Lepanto, breaking their strength for many years after; but the king, Philip II. (the husband of our Mary I.), was jealous of his brother, and called him home, and after that the Venetians were obliged to make peace, and give up Cyprus. The misfortune was that the Greeks and Latins hated each other so much that they never would make common cause heartily against the Turks, and the Greeks did not like to be under Venetian protection; but Venice kept Crete, or Candia, as it was now called, till 1670, when the Turks took it, after a long and terrible siege, lasting more than two years, during which the bravest and most dashing gentlemen of France made a wild expedition to help the Christian cause. But all was in vain; Candia fell, and most of the little isles in the Archipelago came one by one under the cruel power of the Turks.

## CHAP. XLIII. THE VENETIAN CONQUEST AND LOSS. 1684-1796.

Again there was a time of deliverance for Greece. The Turks had had a great defeat before Vienna, and in their weak state the Venetians made another attack on them, and appointed Francis Morosini commander of the fleet and army. He took the little Ionian isle of Sta Maura, and two Albanian towns; and many brave young men, who had read of the glories of ancient Greece in the course of their studies, came from all parts of Europe to fight for her. The governor, or Seraskin, was obliged to retreat, and the Mainots, as the Greeks of the Morea were called, rose and joined him. Corinth, which was as valuable as ever as the door of the peninsula, was taken, and nothing in the Morea remained Turkish but the city of Malvasia. Morosini threw his men into Lepanto, Patras, and pushed on to Athens; but there they had six days' fighting, during which more harm was done to the beautiful old buildings and sculptures than had befallen them in nearly two thousand years of decay. The Turks had shut themselves up in the Acropolis, and made a powder magazine of the Parthenon. A shell from Morosini's batteries fell into it, and blew up the roof, which had remained perfect all these years, and much more damage was done; but the city was won at last, and the Venetians were so much delighted that they chose Morosini Doge, and bestowed on him the surname of Peloponesiacus in honour of his victory. He sent home a great many precious spoils, in the way of old sculptures, to Venice — in especial two enormous marble lions which used to guard the gate of the Piræus, but which now stand on either side of the Arsenal at Venice.

Then he laid siege to Negropont, the chief city of the old isle of Eubœa; but the plague broke out in his camp, and weakened his troops so much that they were defeated and forced to give up the attempt. Illness, too, hindered him from taking Malvasia; his health was broken, and he died soon after his return to Venice. Four great and bloody sea-fights took place during the next few years, and in one the Turks had the victory, in the others it was doubtful; but when peace was made, in the year 1699, the Morea was yielded to the Venetians, and they put a line of forts across the Isthmus to secure it, as in old times. But the Venetian Republic had lost a great deal of strength and spirit, and when, in a few years, the Sultan began to prepare to take back what he had lost, the Doge and Senate paid little attention to his doings; so that, when 100,000 Turks, with the Grand Vizier, sailed against the Morea, besides a fleet of 100 ships, the Venetian commander there had only 8000 men and 19 ships. The Venetians were hopeless, and yielded Corinth after only four days' siege; and though safety had been promised to the inhabitants, they were cruelly massacred, and the same happened in place after place till the whole Morea was conquered, and the Venetians took ship and left the unhappy Greeks to their fate, which was worse than ever, since they were now treated as rebels.

TEMPLE OF MINERVA, ON THE PROMONTORY OF SUNIUM.

Several of the Ionian islands on the west side of Greece were seized by the Turks; but Corfu, the old Corcyra, held out most bravely, the priests, women, and all fighting most desperately as the Turks stormed the walls of their city; stones, iron crosses, everything that came to hand, were hurled down on the heads of the enemy; but the ramparts had been won, and thirty standards planted on the walls, when the Saxon general Schulenberg, who was commanding the Venetians, sallied out with 800 men, and charged the Turks in their rear, so that those on the walls hurried back to defend their camp. At night a great storm swept away the tents, and in the morning a Spanish fleet came to the aid of the island. The Turks were so much disheartened that they embarked as quietly as possible in the night; and when the besieged garrison looked forth in the morning, in surprise at everything being so still and quiet, they found the whole place deserted — stores of powder and food, cannon, wounded men, and all. Corfu has thus never fallen under Turkish power, for in the next year, 1717, a peace was made, in which, though Venice gave up all claim to the Morea, she kept the seven Ionian islands, and they continued under her power as long as she remained a free and independent city — that is to say, till 1796, when she was conquered by the French, and given for a time to Austria.

ANCYRA, GALATIA.

The state of poor Greece was dreadful. The nobles lived in fortresses upon the rocks, and the monks in their fastnesses; but the villages, towns, and coasts were worse off than ever, for the Turks treated them as rebels, and savagely oppressed and misused them. Nor were they united among themselves, for the families who dwelt in the hills were often at deadly feud with each other; the men shot each other down if they met; and it ended in whole families of men living entirely within their castle walls, and never going out except armed to the teeth on purpose to fight, while all the business of life was carried on by the women, whom no one on either side attempted to hurt. The beautiful buildings in the cities were going to decay faster than ever, in especial the Parthenon. When it had lost its roof it was of no further use as a storehouse, so it was only looked on as a mine of white marble, and was broken down on all sides. The English Earl of Elgin obtained leave from the Turkish Government to carry away those carvings from it which are now in the British Museum, and only one row of beautiful pillars from the portico of the Temple has been left standing.

As the Russians had been converted to Christianity by the clergy of Constantinople, and belonged to the same Church, the Greeks naturally looked most there for help; but they were not well treated by the great empire, which seemed to think the chief use of them was to harass the Turks, and keep them from attacking Russia. Thus, in 1770, the Russians sent 2000 men to encourage a rising of the Mainots in the Morea, but not enough to help them to make a real resistance; and the Greeks, when they had a little advantage, were always so horridly cruel in their revenge on their Turkish prisoners as to disgrace the Christian name, and provoke a return. In 1790, again, the Suliot Greeks of Albania sent to invite Constantine, the brother of the Czar of Russia, to be king of Greece, and arranged a rising, but only misery came of it. The Russians only sent a little money, encouraged them to rise, and left them to their fate. The Turkish chief, Ali Pasha, who in his little city of Yanina had almost become a king independent of the Sultan, hunted them down; and the Suliots, taking refuge among the rocks, fought to the death, and killed far more than their own number. In one case the Turks surprised a wedding-party, which retreated to a rock with a precipice behind. Here the women waited and watched till all the men had been slain, and then let themselves be driven over the precipice rather than be taken by the Turks.

## CHAP. XLIV. — THE WAR OF INDEPENDENCE. 1815.

An all their troubles the Greeks never quite lost heart. The merchants who had thriven in trade sent their sons to be educated in France, Russia, and Germany, and these learned to think much of the great old deeds of their forefathers, and they formed a secret society among themselves, called the Hetaira, which in time the princes and nobles of the Peloponnesus joined; so that they felt that if they only were so united and resolute as to make some Christian power think it worth while to take up their cause in earnest, they really might shake off the Turkish yoke.

In 1820, Ali Pasha, the governor of Albania, rebelled, and shut himself up in the town of Yanina, stirring up the Greeks to begin fighting on their own account, so as to prevent the Sultan from using all his power to crush him. So the Greeks began, under Prince Ipsilanti, who had served in the Russian army, to march into the provinces on the Danube; but they were not helped by the Russians, and were defeated by the Turks. Ipsilanti fled into Austria; but another leader, called George the Olympian, lived a wild, outlaw life for some years longer, but as he had no rank the Greeks were too proud to join him. At last he shut himself up in the old convent of Secka, and held it out against the Turks for thirty-six hours, until, finding that he could defend it no longer, he put a match to the powder, and blew himself and his men up in it rather than surrender.

But the next year there was another rising all over Greece. The peasants of Attica drove the Turkish garrison out of all Athens but the Acropolis; the Suliots rose again, with secret encouragement from Ali Pasha, and hope seemed coming back. But when Omar Pasha had been sent from Constantinople with 4000 Turkish troops, he found it only too easy to rout 700 Greeks at Thermopylæ, and, advancing into Attica, he drove back the peasants, and relieved the Turkish garrison in the Acropolis, which had been besieged for eighty-three days; but no sooner had he left the place than the brave peasants returned to the siege.

The worst of the Greeks was that they were very cruel and treacherous, and had very little notion of truth or honour, for people who have been long ground down are apt to learn the vices of slaves; and when the Turks slaughtered the men, burnt the villages, and carried off the women, they were ready to return their savage deeds with the like ferocity, and often with more cunning than the Turks could show; and this made the European nations slow of helping them. In this year, 1821, a Greek captain plotted to set fire to the arsenal at Constantinople, murder the Sultan in the confusion, and begin a great revolt of all the Greeks living at Constantinople. The plot was found out, and terribly visited, for thousands of Christian families, who had never even heard of it, were slain in their houses, and the Patriarch of Constantinople, an aged man, whom everyone loved and respected, was also put to death. Not only were the Christians massacred at Constantinople, but in most of the other large cities of Turkey, and only in a few were the people able to escape on board the Greek merchant ships. These ships carried ten or twelve guns, were small, swift, and well managed, and little fire-ships were sometimes sent by them into the Turkish fleet, which did a great deal of damage.

THE ACROPOLIS, RESTORED.

The slaughter of so many Christians had only enraged instead of terrifying the others; and a Greek prince named Mavrocordato brought an army together, which took several cities, but unhappily was as cruel as the Turks themselves in their treatment of the conquered. However, they now held Argos, met there, and made Mavrocordato their President in 1822. Ali Pasha of Yanina was reduced and shot by the Turks that same year; and Omar Pasha, who had been sent against him, had a great deal of desperate fighting with the Suliots and other Albanian Greeks, but at last he was driven back through the mountains with terrible loss.

Another horrid deed of the Turks did much to turn men's minds against them. There were about 120,000 Christians in the island of Scio, who had taken no part in the war, and only prayed to be let alone; but two Greek captains chose to make an attack on the Turkish garrison, and thus provoked the vengeance of the Turks, who burst in full force on the unhappy island, killed every creature they found in the capital, and ravaged it everywhere. Forty thousand were carried off as slaves, and almost all the rest killed; and when these horrors were over, only 1800 were left in the place.

The cruelty of the Turks and the constancy of the Greeks began to make all Europe take an interest in the war. People began to think them a race of heroes like those of old, and parties of young men, calling themselves Philhellenes, or lovers of Greece, came to fight in their cause. The chief of these was the English poet, Lord Byron; but he, as well as most of the others, found it was much easier to admire the Greeks when at a distance, for a war like this almost always makes men little better than treacherous savage robbers in their ways; and they were all so jealous of one another that there was no obedience to any kind of government, nor any discipline in their armies. Byron soon said he was a fool to have come to Greece, and before he could do anything he died at Missolonghi, in the year 1824. But though the Greeks fought in strange ways of their own, they at least won respect and interest by their untamableness, and though Missolonghi was taken, it was only after a most glorious resistance. When the defenders could hold out no longer, they resolved to cut their way through the Turks. One division of them were deceived by a false alarm, and returned to the town, where, when the enemy entered the powder magazine, they set fire to it, and blew themselves up, together with the Turks; the others escaped.

Athens was taken again by the Turks, all but the Acropolis; but the nations of Europe had begun to believe in the Greeks enough to advance them a large sum of money, which was called the Greek Loan; and the English admiral, Lord Cochrane, and an English soldier, General Church, did them much good by making up the quarrels among their own princes, for actually, in the midst of this desperate war with the Turks, there were seven little civil wars going on among different tribes of the Greeks themselves. General Church collected them all, and fought a great battle in the plain of Athens with the Turkish commander, Ibrahim Pasha, but was beaten again; the Acropolis was taken, and nothing remained to the Greek patriots but the citadel of Corinth and Naupliæ.

However, France, Russia, and England had now resolved to interfere on behalf of the Greeks, and when the Sultan refused to attend to them, a fleet, consisting of ships belonging to the three nations, was sent into the Mediterranean. They meant to treat with the Turks, but the Turks and Greeks thought they meant to fight, and in the bay of Navarino a battle began, which ended in the utter destruction of the Turkish fleet. Out of 120 ships, only 20 or 30 were left, and 6000 men were slain. This was on the 20th of October, 1827, and the terrible loss convinced Ibrahim Pasha that no further attempt to keep the Morea was of any use, so he sailed away to Egypt, of which his father was then Viceroy for the Sultan, but which he and his son have since made into a separate kingdom. It was in October, 1828, that the Peloponnesus thus shook off the Turkish yoke.

It was thought best that a French army should be sent to hold the chief fortresses in the Morea, because the Greeks quarrelled so among themselves. In the meantime General Church went on driving the Turks back in the northern parts of Greece, and Count Capo d'Istria was chosen President, but he did not manage well, and gave the command of Western Greece to his own dull brother, taking it away from General Church. It seemed as if the Greeks would not know how to use their freedom now they had gained it, for the Council and the President were always quarrelling, and being jealous of each other; and there was falsehood, robbery, treachery, and assassination everywhere. And yet everyone hoped that the race that had stood so bravely all these years would improve now it was free.

## CHAP. XLV. — THE KINGDOM OF GREECE. 1822–1875.

The European powers who had taken the little nation of Greeks in charge, finding that, as a republic with a president, they did nothing but dispute and fight, insisted that the country should have a king, who should govern by the help of a parliament.

But the difficulty was that nobody had any claim to be king, and the Greeks were all so jealous of each other that there was no chance of their submitting to one of themselves. The only royal family belonging to their branch of the Church were the Russians; and France, England, Austria, and all the rest were afraid of letting the great Russian power get such a hold on the Mediterranean Sea as would come of Greece being held by one of the brothers or sons of the Czar. The first choice was very wise, for it was of one of the fittest men in Europe, Prince Leopold of Saxe Coburg; and he accepted their offer at first, but when he had had time to hear more in letters from Count Capo d'Istrias, and found what a dreadful state the country was in, and how little notion the people had of truth, honour, orobedience, he thought he should be able to do nothing with them, and refused to come to Greece. In the meantime the Greeks went on worse than ever. Capo d'Istrias was murdered by the son and brother of a chief whom he had imprisoned; and two bodies of men met, each calling itself a National Assembly — one at Argos, the other at Megara — and there was a regular civil war, during which the poor peasants had to hide in the woods and caves.

At last, in 1832, the second son of the king of Bavaria, Otho, a lad of seventeen, was chosen king by the conference in London which was settling the affairs of Greece. He was sent with a council to rule for him till he should be of age, and with a guard of Bavarian soldiers, while the French troops were sent home again; but the Ionian islands remained under the British protection, and had an English Lord High Commissioner, and garrisons of English troops.

Otho had been chosen so young that there might be the better chance of his becoming one with his subjects, but he turned out very dull and heavy, and caused discontent, because he gave all the offices he could dispose of to his German friends rather than to Greeks, which perhaps was the less wonderful that it was very hard to find a Greek who could be trusted. At last, in 1843, the people rose upon him, forced him to send away all his Bavarians, and to have Greek ministers to manage the government, who should be removed at the will of the people.

His capital was at Athens, and as everyone wished to see the places which had been made glorious by the great men of old Greece, there was such a resort of travellers thither as soon to make the town flourish; but the Government was so weak, and the whole people so used to a wild, outlaw life, that the country still swarms everywhere with robbers, whom the peasants shelter and befriend in spite of their many horrid crimes.

THE ISLES OF GREECE.

When the English and French nations, in the year 1853, took up the cause of Turkey against Russia, the Greeks much longed to have fought against their old enemies; but the two allied nations sent a strong guard to Athens, and kept them down. Otho had no children, and time did not draw him and his people nearer together; and after a reign of about thirty years, it was plain that the experiment had not succeeded. He resigned, and went home to end his days in Bavaria.

The Greek crown was offered to several more princes, who refused it, until George, the second son of the king of Denmark, accepted it in the year 1868. At the same time the Ionian islands were made over by the English Government to the crown of Greece, and the British troops withdrawn. One of the first things that happened in King George's reign was the murder of three English gentlemen — Mr. Herbert, Mr. Lloyd, and Mr. Vyner — who had gone with a party to see the plain of Marathon. A gang of robbers came and seized upon them and carried them off to the hills, demanding a ransom. Lady Muncaster, who was of the party, was allowed to return to Athens with her husband, the robbers intending that the ransom should be collected; but troops were sent out to rescue the prisoners, and in rage and disappointment the robbers shot them all three. The robbers were captured and put to death, and the young king was bitterly grieved at not having been able to prevent these horrors.

PLAIN OF MARATHON.

Schools are doing what they can, and the Greeks are very quick-witted, and learn easily. They are excellent sailors, clever merchants, and ready linguists, and they get on and prosper very fast; but till they learn truth, honesty, and mercy, and can clear their country of robbers, it does not seem as if anything could go really well with their kingdom, or as if it could make itself be respected. Yet we must recollect that the old Eastern Empire, under which they were for many centuries, did not teach much uprightness or good faith; and that since that time they have had four hundred years of desperate fighting for their homes and their creed with a cruel and oppressive enemy, and that they deserve honour for their constancy even to the death. Let us hope they will learn all other virtues in time.

## NOTES.

[1] "E" and "o" marked thus (ê) (ô) are pronounced long, as "Helleens."

[2] Thessaly, Epirus, Acarnania, Ætolia, Doris, two Locrian states, Phocis, Bœotia, Attica, Megaris — Corinth, Sicyon, Phliasia, Achaia, Elis, Arcadia, Argolis, Laconia, Messenia